THE Love List

OF A LIFETIME

Praise for *The Love List of a Lifetime*

"*The Love List of a Lifetime* isn't your typical end-of-life planner. What sets Sherry apart is her remarkable ability to infuse everything she creates with love and joy, even when addressing life's most difficult moments. While the end-of-life experience is undeniably profound and often painful, Sherry reminds us that the tools and materials we use to navigate it don't have to be morbid. Instead, they can be vibrant, uplifting, and deeply human."

—Brad Wolfe, founder and executive director of Reimagine

"*The Love List of a Lifetime* is a wonderful and essential guide to one of life's most important tasks. Preparing for one's end of life is daunting, but Sherry Belul is a skillful and compassionate companion for the journey. Let her big heart and creative mind support you to leave behind a lasting legacy."

—Roy Remer, executive director of Zen Caregiving Project

"*The Love List of a Lifetime* is a gentle and practical guide to preparing for aging, illness, and end of life. People often wonder, 'Why prepare for death, I'll be dead.' The author explains the many whys in such a compelling way and serves as a kind and knowledgeable guide for readers as they embark upon the beautiful gift of death preparation."

—Lisa Pahl, creator of *The Death Deck*

"Death and taxes are inevitable. Fortunately, there are accountants to help with taxes. But no one really prepares us for dealing with death and dying. That is, until now with this much-needed end-of-life planner. What makes this book so special and so wonderful is that it imparts what could be a difficult task with lots of love. As a result, what might be a chore turns into an incredible gift for you and your loved ones."

—Allen Klein, author of *Embracing Life After Loss*

"A well-prepared gift, meal, holiday, or event is an intentional and genuine act of kindness. Yet, so many people wander willy-nilly into their last days. While no one lives forever, it's tempting to behave as if we do. In her characteristic style of kindness and celebration, Sherry Belul makes preparing for the ultimate exit the ultimate gift of grace. This book puts a punctuation mark of peace on the many paragraphs of our living days."

—Mary Anne Radmacher, artist, speaker, and author of *Live with Intention* and *Courage Doesn't Always Roar*

THE
Love List
OF A LIFETIME

YOUR ESSENTIAL END-OF-LIFE PLANNER
with Practical Notes and Instructions
for the Loved Ones You Leave Behind

Sherry Richert Belul

Books That Save Lives

Cover Design: Joanna Price, joannapricedesign.com
Layout & Design: Carmen Fortunato

Published by BTSL/Jim Dandy Publishing
6252 Peach Avenue
Van Nuys, CA 91411
info@jimdandypublishing.com

For bulk orders, special quantities, course adoptions, and corporate sales,
please email info@jimdandypublishing.com

ISBN: 978-1-68481-699-6
BISAC: LAW / Right to Die

Printed in the United States of America

Dedication

For Scott McKenney with heartfelt gratitude for championing the importance of this book's message—your belief made all the difference.

And also for Lisa Myers, whose life beautifully embodied the ideas and values of this book—your light continues to inspire the world and bring these pages to life.

I wish you were both here to witness the impact of your unwavering support and love.

Table of Contents

Foreword

The Love List of a Lifetime is the end-of-life planner I've been searching for. As an attorney, estate planning has been an essential part of my personal tool kit. I understand, however, that wills, trusts, powers of attorney, and advance directives only scratch the surface of what is needed to assist your loved ones in wrapping up your affairs.

I come from a long line of planners. Both my parents wanted their ducks in a row when their time came and left me with a prearranged and prepaid funeral and internment plan. This thoughtful detail made the process exponentially easier for me.

My grandmother employed a simpler sort of planning. She labeled all the family heirlooms with pieces of masking tape, each bearing the name of the person who she wanted to have the item after her death. I vividly remember helping her pull out the good china, silver, and crystal every Thanksgiving. We'd remove the masking tape labels and line them up on the windowsill over the kitchen sink. When the meal was over and the dishes washed and dried, I'd replace these labels under her careful supervision. She lived a long life, so we performed this ritual for many years. It taught me at an early age that planning for your death isn't morbid, but a kindness to those left behind.

Under the expert guidance of Sherry Richert Belul, *The Love List of a Lifetime* leads us through this process. She covers the legal, financial, and business-y aspects of end-of-life planning. Ms. Belul's genius, however, is that she also challenges us to capture and convey our emotional legacy to our loved ones. We all have stories, emotions, and wisdom that we can and should leave behind. These ephemeral assets are often what is more valuable to and treasured by our loved ones.

Examining one's own life is a joyful and affirming process. It helps us to be mindful of how we're spending our precious time and intentional about where we're focusing our energies. In *The Love List of a Lifetime*, Ms. Belul accompanies us on this journey with kindness, compassion, and great insight. A task that might seem morbid, hard, or cold is mindful and joyful under her talented supervision. As you embark on this process, I hope you find it as life-affirming as I have.

—Barbara Hinske, *USA Today* bestselling author

Introduction

"Talking about death brings me to life."
—Sherry R. Belul

We're on This Journey Together

This Book Is a Gift to Your Loved Ones—and to Yourself

Hello, my friend. I realize we don't yet know one another; however, this is the beginning of a powerful and important journey together. I'm certain we will be good friends during these travels.

I care about you. I can say this despite the fact that we've never met, because you are here, reading a book about planning for your end of life. Since you are doing this, you must be someone with a good heart who cares deeply for the people in your life. I know that you are someone who is responsible and who wants to make sure your life (or death) isn't a burden on anyone.

Whether you've been given this book or have chosen to purchase it, you are here, reading, with at least some amount of interest and willingness. For that, I honor you and appreciate you.

Here's the most important thing I want you to know: The process you are about to embark upon is the greatest gift you can give to people in your life—and to yourself.

On the outside, it may look like a whole lot of paperwork, plans, and legal mumbo jumbo. You will be asked to reflect on a lot of things. This process may look challenging or daunting. Maybe it sounds scary or sad to you. But its essence is peace of mind and deep love.

You are setting the stage to leave your loved ones as much ease and tranquility as possible in the wake of grief. You are doing something that may be a challenge for you; and you are doing it selflessly in order to make life easier on the people you love.

Just as importantly, every step of the way, I promise you will feel a greater lightness and clarity about your life. You will find more meaning; you will reconnect to your life in the most surprising of ways.

The beautiful irony of this end-of-life planner is that it will bring you straight home to the heart of your life.

If you are willing to trust me and this process, I know you will come to feel more alive than perhaps ever before.

You don't have to believe me right now.

I will be guiding you and enthusiastically beckoning you along. If you follow and take action a little at a time, over time, you will feel the joy of this process.

I'll Be with You Every Step of the Way

Since we are embarking upon this intimate journey together, I want to know a little about me.

I'm an author, coach, and founder of Simply Celebrate, a company dedicated to helping people celebrate everyday life and the people we love.

I wrote a book called *Say It Now*, which offers creative and meaningful ways to show our love and appreciation to our family and friends.

Thus, you can see that my career has been about celebrating life and letting other people know we love them. This book does both. This is the last, most loving gift we can give loved ones. And it is also one of the most extraordinary journeys, one that will help us appreciate and celebrate our own life.

I'm excited to bring you a legacy planner that is different from all the others—one that will not only help you leave behind all the important information needed by your family, but will also be a way for you to create a treasury for them, too.

Why This Process Is So Important for You and Your Loved Ones

In my spiritual tradition, there is a phrase we use: "Leave not a trace." Generally, what this means is that we are mindful about cleaning up after ourselves and always leaving places exactly as we found them. It is a way to show respect for the next people to come along. For instance, it may be the simple act of putting away all of the dishes and wiping down the counters after using the kitchen. It might be sweeping off the porch before leaving a woodsy cabin.

In nature, this concept encourages us to pack out our trash and to be mindful of extinguishing all of our campfires. We want to leave the landscape as pristine as we found it so anyone arriving after us can enjoy the beauty, just as we did.

You could look at this book as a similar process. We can be thoughtful about leaving behind a sense of sweet peace after we have completed our travels on this planet.

In the same way that most people would never think, "Who cares—I'm never coming back to this park," as they leave their trash scattered everywhere on the trail, we also don't want to think, "Well, I'll be gone, so I don't have to think about the many details, legalities, and actual stuff I will be leaving behind after I die."

But just like with that trash on the trail, someone *will* be cleaning up after you. And if you have close family or friends whom you love, that is who will be doing this work.

As you go through this process, you might imagine if it were your spouse, child, or best friend who would be staying at that campsite or walking that trail after you. How could you make things the most peaceful and easy for them?

Getting Clear on Your Own Why

No matter how challenging, daunting, or even sad it might feel at this moment to think about and plan the end of your life and what will happen after you die, the one thing that will make it all possible—and dare I say, enjoyable—is remembering *why* you are going through the process: this truly is the last gift you will ever give the people you love.

It can be so stressful for people not to know where to find information or what their loved one's wishes were once that person has died. This adds a further layer of stress to the grief, one that can be avoided with a book like this. As well, this is a chance to remember to express your love, gratitude, and wisdom learned from this lifetime.

The most surprising aspect of completing an end-of-life planner like this is it will help you feel more alive right now. This is a growth journey and vitality practice, as well as a last gift.

I know for myself, I can't think about mortality without wondering, "How am I living? How am I loving? If this life is finite—which I can pretty much be guaranteed that it is—what matters most in the time I have left?"

Sometimes having to face the fact that our lives are limited might be the greatest gift we can ever receive. We stop thinking we have all the time in the world. We stop putting things off. We clean up our relationships, we get clear on our spiritual or religious beliefs, and we put our affairs in order.

These things will bring you a profound sense of peace on many levels.

We've created a worksheet for you that's at the end of this section. It will help you stay connected to your why.

☀️ EXPERT TIP:

Focus on the People You Love

"It is a loving gift to prepare ahead of time. Some of it is about the ease of having things in order, but mostly it is for the emotional well-being of the grievers.

Working in hospice, I provide bereavement calls to check how family members are doing after their loved one has died. It's night and day depending on whether there were preparations in advance. The stress of handling death tasks is overwhelming, and there's often anger: 'You left me all this stuff, and now I can't even grieve because I'm on the phone with the bank about an account I didn't know you had.'

I think it's a bit selfish when we don't prepare because we are thinking, 'It doesn't matter; I'll be dead.'"

—Lisa Pahl, hospice/ER social worker and cocreator of *The Death Deck*

Always Remember You Are Not Alone

The reason I wanted to write this book is because I have been through this process. I know how daunting it may seem. *And*, I have so much respect, admiration, and compassion for anyone who is willing to say *yes* to this process. I want to be your loving guide and your friend along the way.

Additionally, as you read through this book, you will see that dozens of others have weighed in on the process—experts and everyday people who have traveled this path and who want to share what they've learned with you. They, too, are your guides.

I've been intentional about including many resources in the back of this book. You'll see that they are organized by section. So anytime you feel stuck or need an additional hand, simply flip to the back of the book, look for the corresponding section, and you will find help.

📱 Scan Me

You are not alone: getting started

📱 Scan Me

Resource Directory

Getting Started—One Small Step at a Time

Start Early. Go Slowly. Be Gentle

This can be a daunting process. We encourage you to tiptoe through it as it unfolds and go at your own pace. This is why it is so important to start *now*—hopefully before you are ill or have a terminal prognosis.

Don't worry. I will guide you to the most important aspects and help you know where to start and how to get help, so no matter where you are on this journey, you can prioritize.

How the Book Is Organized and How to Use It

This book has been carefully and lovingly organized for you in the sequence that may bring you the most peace of mind the quickest. You'll notice that the legal practicalities are first, followed by funeral plans, household issues, and other practical matters that will bring great relief to those left behind.

You know how I mentioned the phrase "Leave not a trace"? That sense of leaving everything in order is just one part of this process. Another part of this process is all about "Leave a loving footprint." The second half of the book helps you navigate some essential emotional and relationship matters.

This book is a guide filled with questions and checklists. You won't be able to store your important paperwork in this book, of course—you will likely have some notarized legal papers and some digital files. That's okay! You will see that there are some places in the book for you to write down where things can be found. Please do this! When your next of kin picks up the book and flips through it, it will help them immensely to quickly identify where you have saved important information.

🔍 USEFUL TOOLS:
Set Up a File Box

Designate a Pendaflex file box to store all of your printed documents and any notes, letters, or historical memorabilia. You may choose to keep these hanging folders in a fireproof box or a fireproof/waterproof safe. I purchased a set of files made by a company called Nokbox, which included an entire system that made this process feel streamlined and simple. I found that simply setting up the box gave me a sense of forward movement. Then, every time I filed a document in the box, I felt a sense of progress. I knew my family would easily be able to flip through the folders to find what they needed after my period of passing. Even the empty folders would be useful clues for my family if I unexpectedly died tomorrow: my next of kin would know that I had not been able to get to that part of the planning process.

Consider This: Sometimes Fear Is Just a Childhood Monster Under the Bed

I talked to a really great teacher and coach, Paul Wesselmann, who has been through some very hard emotional stuff in his life. When we were talking about ways people can feel more comfortable with this death planning process, here's something Paul said based on his experience and that of the people he has supported:

> There are a lot of good reasons why people are afraid of dying. Many of them may be traumas from the past that we've locked away. Scary stuff happened, and then we blocked it so far out of sight that it became this monster under the bed. We are afraid to look, even now, as adults.

> But sometimes when we think we can't do something, that's exactly the reason to look a little closer and ask, "Why does this scare me so much? Could there be something here that will help me understand myself a little better, or perhaps help me to let go of something, or maybe help me grow a bit?"

> It's quite possible that looking where I am terrified could be exactly the thing that will help me die better.

I love that. Imagine our lives without that monster under the bed! There's freedom waiting on the other side whenever we're afraid of something and we face it.

The Love List of a Lifetime

Maybe there are some hard relationships that we haven't dealt with, or a feeling of regret around parts of our lives, or perhaps we are afraid of a painful death. Whatever those monsters are, now's the time to face them. There are a lot of things we can't control, and there are many things we may choose to simply accept. But I bet that in a lot of cases, there are actually some things we can do to help ourselves be ready.

I remember how scared I was about giving birth. I had heard so many horror stories and didn't know what to expect. How painful or unbearable might it be? I couldn't control what the birth would be like, just like I can't control what my death will be.

However, there were a lot of things I could do in preparation to give myself the best chance of an easier birthing process. I could eat really healthy foods and do a lot of yoga. I could meditate and learn how to be with myself through hard times. All of those things are also things we can do if we are willing to turn and face the I'm-afraid-of-death monsters head on.

That reminds me of a powerful quote by Viktor Frankl: "When we are no longer able to change a situation, we are challenged to change ourselves." Frankl was a Holocaust survivor and the author of *Man's Search for Meaning*.

·ᗡ́- EXPERT TIP:

Be Patient with Yourself and Go Slowly

"Statistics suggest that approximately 100 percent of people are going to die. Some of us are going to be better prepared or have an easier time than others. Since it's inevitable that we're going to die, what if we ask, 'How could we make it easier and better for ourselves and also easier on the people whom we care about?' Maybe all of this death talk scares the bejesus out of us. That's okay. We tiptoe. We go carefully. We hold hands with someone who will help us figure it out all."

—Paul Wesselmann, The Ripples Guy

Consider This: Every Step You Take Benefits the People You Love

I can only imagine that you may be thinking, "What?! She said to create a whole filing system? This sounds like a part-time job. This is daunting and terrible. I don't want to immerse myself in this depressing process. I thought this could take a couple hours and then I'd be done."

I get it. But here's the thing: Every single step you take relieves some anxiety or stress on the people left behind. I mean this. Every individual thing you organize now saves your loved one two or three times the amount of time because you are working within the familiar context of your own life. Your loved ones will be trying to piece things together in the midst of grief.

So, I encourage you to think of the process as a stress-reducing one. Every document you complete or action you take is a success. Truly!

Imagine if you wanted to lose fifty pounds. It would be daunting to imagine changing your diet, increasing exercise, improving your mindset, and buying new clothes all at once. You don't need to! Maybe you would start by simply adding a vegetable to your meal each day or drinking more water. Small, simple steps *will* get you to your goal. This is the same process.

Instead of focusing on how much there is to do in this process, keep focusing on the positives of every small step.

Celebrate Yourself!

Remember at the start of this section when I talked about people leaving trash along the trail that others have to clean up? Well, right now, you are the good-hearted person grabbing a checklist and a plastic bag, all set to look around and make sure you are not leaving a mess for anyone else to clean up. I hope you will pause and celebrate this!

You've done a lot simply by showing up with the willingness to explore this process.

I've left you a little something at the end of this section to help you celebrate where you are and to encourage you to keep going.

I'm celebrating you

☑ Introduction Worksheet: Checklist and Fill In

Defining Your Why Will Help Make the Journey Happier

Read over this list and circle as many of these "whys" as apply to you. When you have done so, please write your specific loving reminders to yourself on the lines below this list. Add anything that may be part of your *why* that we didn't list. Then bookmark this page so you can return to it anytime you feel overwhelmed or a little unwilling.

- I want my loved ones not to feel stress, but simply be able to grieve.
- I want there to be harmony and clear communication for my family.
- I want my final wishes to be known and followed, if possible.
- I want to leave a written legacy of my life.
- I would rather face a little overwhelm myself in order to alleviate it after my death for people I love. (Better me than them!)
- I want peace of mind for having done this process.
- I want to feel lighter for the remaining days or years of my life.
- I trust that this process will bring me unexpected joy.
- I like feeling responsible and caring for things that are my duty.
- I like the idea of not leaving a trace.
- I like the idea of being intentional about my legacy.
- I feel like this is a moral, financial, or ethical responsibility.
- This process will give me a way to talk about death with people I love.
- I want to be a role model for others in living my best life and dying my best, too.
- I want to live the rest of my life with peace and compassion, knowing I have loved the best I can.

My Why:

_____

_____

_____

These Actions Are Your Legacy of Love

"We will do for the love of others what we won't do for ourselves."
—Cheri Huber, Zen teacher

Love Will Guide the Way

You Can Do This; I Promise!

In the Cheri Huber quote on the previous page, the clarity of her Zen Buddhist wisdom comes shining through.

Cheri is right, isn't she? Isn't it true that throughout our lives, we are willing (and able!) to do uncomfortable or hard things for the people we love? When we love someone, we can persevere through almost any challenge in order to save them pain or grief.

If you have children, you likely remember getting up at all hours of the night when they were newborns so you could feed them when they woke up wailing. You changed diapers, wiped away spit-up, and suffered through many public tantrums because you truly love those little beings.

If you don't have children, perhaps you've loved a furry friend who has shared a household with you. You've been willing to go through many difficult, time-consuming, sometimes yucky, and often expensive endeavors to take the best care you can of that companion.

I know that you've practically walked through fire for your friends, as well. You've taken them to the airport at the crack of dawn, you've stayed by their bedside when they were sick, you've attended funerals of people they love to show your support.

My friend, *that* is the attitude of mind I want you to summon for the tasks ahead of you that I will be outlining in this section.

This Is Your Chance to Bring Ease as Part of Your Legacy

Lots of people avoid thinking about the end of life or planning for it. Of course, there are many valid and understandable reasons for this, but the result is that their death may unintentionally cause an even greater grief in those left behind. It may also trigger anger, frustration, financial woes, and broken family ties.

I've spoken to countless people as I've been writing this book. It seems like everyone has at least one traumatic story (if not many!) about a close friend or family member who became gravely ill or who passed away without adequate planning—and it resulted in confusion and suffering. Those left behind were left to deal with all of the logistics of illness and death, while also caring for or grieving someone they deeply loved.

It can be especially stressful not to know where to find your loved one's Health Care Directive or any indication of their wishes for burial or cremation location. Often family members don't even know *if* there is a will   or if there is, where to find it. Homes and assets are commonly tied up in probate court, sometimes for years—meaning that assets are frozen.

This section of the planning process is your chance to gift loved ones a different experience, one that shows you were intentional in easing the burden of the logistics so that they could do the most necessary work: that of love and grief.

We are beginning one of the necessary aspects of end-of-life planning: creating legal documents like the ones listed on the following pages.

Medical and Financial Must-Have Forms

These Legal Documents Will Make a Huge Difference

This planner provides a checklist of important end-of-life legal documents and resources to help you find and complete them.

Although there can be much more to planning and organizing for our end of life and legacy, we are starting here because these are the most important things to do. If you complete the items in this section, you will already be offering a significant gift to your loved ones.

To encourage you, I want to share a common scenario that San Francisco realtor Cynthia Cummins recounted:

> I've been with siblings who've inherited a house. They're standing around—kind of scratching their heads—going, "What did mom want? What should we do now?" They start looking all over for clues, and then one says, "Well, I think she wanted this." And the other one says, "Well, I'm pretty sure she wanted that." Nobody ever had a direct conversation about it, so they're left to wonder and never know.

It can be quite traumatic to deal with these logistical uncertainties, especially during such a hard time.

It's likely you've heard of families who have struggled greatly because the documents that you are about to complete were not in place. I want you to know that when it comes to your legacy, making sure these legal documents are in place will provide deep peace to your loved ones in the weeks and months after you are gone.

Taking care of this will help relieve so much stress, frustration, and anxiety for the people you leave behind. And you will be happily surprised at the amount of relief *you* will feel simply by having them completed and filed away!

- **Advance Health Care Directive/Living Will:** This is a legal document that outlines your preferences for medical treatments such as life support in case you become unable to communicate. It is important to appoint a Health Care Proxy, a trusted person to make health care decisions on your behalf.

- **General and Durable Power of Attorney (POA) for Health Care:** General POA (effective immediately) and durable POA (remains effective if you become incapacitated).

- **Will:** A will ensures your assets are distributed according to your wishes. It can appoint guardians for minor children, pets, or other dependents.

- **Trust:** Trusts are commonly used in estate planning to manage assets, reduce taxes, and ensure that assets are distributed according to the grantor's wishes. A trust may be optional, depending on your assets. But please talk to an attorney to see what they think. You most definitely want to avoid probate if you can since it is time-intensive and can be costly for your next of kin.

We've listed other legal forms you may want to complete on your worksheet at the end of this section. However, the four that I've just noted above will go a long way to creating ease for you and your family.

PLEASE NOTE that I am not a lawyer and this is not legal advice! Every person's financial, health, and legal needs will be different depending on their individual situation. Please consult with an attorney in your state who specializes in estate planning to ensure you are meeting legal requirements.

Consider This: DIY Legal Forms May or May Not Be Best for You

Everyone's assets and legal situations are unique, so it isn't possible for me to tell you whether to hire an attorney or to take the do-it-yourself route.

You can choose to complete these legal documents yourself using an online resource such as LegalZoom, Rocket Lawyer, or Nolo; however, just like with our taxes, each of us needs to assess our situation to think about how basic or complicated it is.

I can give you a guiding hand by saying that the more complex your income and assets, the more likely it is you will need to hire an attorney. The higher your net worth or the more complicated your family situation, the more likely you will want a professional to help!

In fact, I talked to Flavia Berys, an attorney who does estate planning, and she wanted me to remind you that aside from net worth, "Attorneys will consider if it is a first or second marriage or if you are single. Are you making an estate plan for one person or jointly for a married couple? They will also ask you, is this a blended family? Do you have an ex-spouse to support? Children from another relationship?" She adds, "The more complicated your situation is, the more time it takes for an attorney to create your estate plan."

Flavia also gave me some other helpful tips. Check out the sidebar on the next page where she outlines how essential an estate plan is. While you are reading these, weigh for yourself what will work best for you and if you should invest in expert assistance.

Should you choose to go the DIY route of using an online set of forms and then having them notarized, we encourage you to consult with legal and financial professionals to ensure that your plan aligns with the laws where you live and that they were completed accurately.

No matter which route you choose—DIY or hiring an attorney—I hope you will remember that the best time to complete these forms is as soon as possible. No matter what stage of life you are in, it will serve your family to have these documents ready just in case something unforeseen should happen.

I hope you live a long and healthy life—and having these plans in place, even as early as in your thirties or forties, will make those long years feel even more peaceful!

💡 EXPERT TIP:

Completing Your Estate Plan Will Leave You Feeling Great in Many Ways

I've heard so many people say they don't need to do estate planning because, as their line goes, "This is too much. I won't care about any of this when I'm gone anyway." So, I asked an attorney to outline the main reasons she might encourage someone to make these legal forms a priority in life.

Here's what she said:

1. The top reason to complete your estate planning is to relieve the trauma and stress that your next of kin would go through if you were to pass away in a disorganized way. It's not only the saddest thing, but also very confusing and frustrating for them. The organization that estate planning forces you to do is really for the people you love.

2. The second reason is an economic one. Transferring wealth from one generation to the next can be done in ways that provide tax advantages and bypass the time-consuming probate process.

3. The third reason is having control over what happens to the people and things you care about—beloved pets, children and other dependents, or belongings—and directing how they are taken care of, by whom, and in what manner. Without a plan, you have no way to have a say in this.

4. The fourth reason is privacy. When an estate plan is set up properly, much of what happens after you pass is handled privately, out of the public eye. If you pass away without an estate plan, your assets and possessions may end up in a probate court case for public view. This can feel embarrassing to your heirs and next of kin. Do you really want everyone to know your net worth and who got what? A structured estate plan keeps private things private.

5. The fifth reason is your own peace of mind. Sure, estate planning can feel like a heavy lift at the beginning, with the lawyer asking you to research and list all your assets, bank accounts, retirement accounts, and so on. It feels like homework, and it is easy to procrastinate. That's understandable. But once it's done, people always feel lighter and more at peace. People realize they have let go of a huge stress they never even knew they had.

—Flavia Berys, estate planning and real estate attorney

Consider This: Complete These Forms for Your Young Adult Children

As I've been writing this book, I've been talking to everyone I meet about their legacy planning. The other day at my Zumba class, I mentioned it to my friend Carolyn. She told me something I didn't know, and I am passing it along to you because this could be essential in preventing a lot of stress in your family.

Carolyn said she'd received a newsletter from Charles Schwab which included a reminder that if we have *children who are over eighteen years old*, we are encouraged to complete these three legal forms:

- **Health Insurance Portability and Accountability Act (HIPAA) Authorization:** Parents need a HIPAA release, otherwise health care providers cannot share anything about our adult children's health with us.

- **Health Care Proxy or Durable Medical Power of Attorney (POA):** This document allows parents to make medical decisions on behalf of your adult child if necessary.

- **Financial POA:** This document allows you to access your adult child's financial records and make financial decisions in case something happens to them.

While these are technically not legal forms for *you*, having such forms completed by your adult children can be important for your family's future well-being and peace. If you are already in the process of notarizing documents and filing them in an organized way, and you have young adult children who are unmarried, I highly encourage you to include these.

Keep in mind that the decision of whether or not to create and sign these legal documents is *entirely* up to your adult child who is aged eighteen or over. Persuasion rather than pressure is likely to be what will work. Perhaps as a step to building consensus, it would be a good idea to give them (either on paper or electronically) copies of the blank forms and written explanations of the benefits of each. If they balk at the notion, you may want to table the discussion and come back to it at a later time. Events in a younger adult's life, such as the loss of a friend to tragedy, can open their eyes to the need to prepare for the unexpected.

Be open to the possibility that they may want to designate someone as the holder of their medical, financial, and/or general power of attorney who is not you (nor perhaps their other parent).

Make sure you talk to your estate planning attorney about making sure these forms get done. Alternatively, if you are using a DIY online site, search for these while you are completing other forms.

I was easily able to find these forms online, sit down with my twenty-four-year-old son while he was home on break, fill them out, and then get them notarized. They are filed away in my Nokbox, where I could grab them at a moment's notice if need be. I can't imagine how stressful it would be if something happened to him and his dad and I didn't have any say in my son's care.

Don't forget: I have provided some wonderful resources for you at the back of this book! Look for the resources marked "Section 1: Legacy of Love" for a wealth of support.

It's Time to Bring Others into Your Legacy Plan

Conversations Give Context to Your Legal Forms and Allow Your Loved Ones to Share Their Thoughts

As you are working on some of these legal forms, you will likely find that there are places where you want to have conversations with your next of kin—particularly about the Advance Health Care Directive, which would greatly impact your loved ones if you were to become gravely ill or incapacitated.

Grief specialist Cheryl Espinosa Jones confessed that she had to take a pause while finishing up her own medical directive. "Not because I'm afraid of death—but because I care deeply about how my choices affect the people who will grieve me," she said. "Two of my children don't live around here, and I want to make sure they have the opportunity to travel to see me if I'm in a condition I can't recover from. So, I realized I can't just check the 'pull the plug' box. I need to include additional directives to support my kids' needs."

She added, "I encourage you to bring your family into the planning process so you can hear how they feel and include their wishes whenever possible. We used the Five Wishes questions to prompt deeper—dare I say, more sacred—conversations about some of the choices."

It can be difficult to talk to our families, either in the process of finalizing these legal documents or once they are completed. I understand! This may be a topic that has been ignored—or even taboo—in your family. After all, none of us want to think about a time when we won't be here any longer or when someone we love will be gone.

Trust me, though. Opening up these conversations will build a greater depth of intimacy, gratitude, and understanding in your family.

Make sure you take a look at the resources for this section. You can find a link to Five Wishes as well as to many other very helpful organizations.

❤️🔍 USEFUL TOOLS:

This Card Game Opens Up Conversation

I love that you are completing all of the legal paperwork to support your next of kin. I want to remind you that it is also important to have conversations about these legalities with your loved ones so they don't second-guess any of your written directives.

I found an amazing resource and used it with my own family. It is called *The Death Deck* and is a simple and rather playful card game that makes talking about this stuff easier.

The cocreator of the deck shared with me a little about why conversations matter. She said:

"I've worked in hospice for seventeen years, and I've also worked in the ER for eight years. In both settings, almost no one is prepared for medical crises. It's not unusual for eighty-five-year-olds to come into the ER with no advance directive, and the family couldn't respond to any of the staff's questions, leading to terrible arguments in the hospital room. It doesn't have to be this hard.

If I'm in a situation where I can't speak for myself, my husband might not know the answer to everything, but we've had many conversations about how I feel, and I've been explicit in my writing about not wanting aggressive treatments. I know he might face pushback, but I've told him to stay strong because this is how I feel.

Writing things down is helpful, but what I find professionally and in my own life is that the conversations give us the confidence to make decisions for our family members. A meaningful conversation is memorable."

—Lisa Pahl, hospice/ER social worker and cocreator of *The Death Deck*

Consider This: Drop the Superstitions and Free Yourself from Fear

Don't feel bad if you are someone who feels a little superstitious about filling out these forms and putting all the legalities in place. It is so common!

However, Cheryl Espinosa Jones encourages us to flip our thinking: "Many people are afraid of doing this work. I hear it over and over. They don't want to complete their end-of-life plans because there's a superstitious belief that doing so will invite death. But the truth is, it's quite the opposite. Nothing has freed me to live more than facing the idea of my death. And many others have expressed this same sentiment. It is the opposite of what we think!"

Consider This: You Can Infuse This Process with Meaning

This process can be challenging, but you are doing it. I hope you can recognize the deep importance of taking action. I also hope that you will continue to seek support along the way.

There's a wonderful organization called Reimagine, which is all about championing new ways to support people at the end of life with a heart-centered approach. Reimagine hosts workshops and conversations from countless collaborators all over the world. Many of their offerings are on a donation basis or sliding scale to make them accessible.

Brad Wolfe, founder of Reimagine, says:

> There are so many incredible services and organizations focused on transforming the end of life. But most are logistical and underutilized because people avoid talking about death until it's right on their doorstep. By then, emotional overwhelm leaves little room to explore these options.
>
> What's missing is a connection to what death is really about. Yes, logistics matter, but at its core, our end-of-life experience is a heart-centered journey. It's about what matters most: the meaning of life, the people we care about, and the parts of living that deeply connect to our emotions.

He's right. If we can remember to connect this process to what matters most, it will give us the courage and energy we need.

-☼- EXPERT TIP:
Talking About Endings Can Bring Us an Unexpected Depth of Gratitude

"Taking the time to think about mortality is enlivening and enhances the way we live our lives. That may sound surprising, but when we turn toward endings, whether it's the end of life or simply the end of this conversation, it brings us to a place of gratitude.

Gratitude fires up all the reward centers in the brain, which makes us feel really, really good. It's biological, not just an emotional perspective. So, if we can take the time to think about our own eventual passing—or the death of a partner, a parent, or a friend—it orients our thinking toward what we appreciate about ourselves, our lives, or those people."

—Roy Remer, executive director of Zen Caregiving Project

Celebrate All of Your Hard Work

I want you to know how amazing you are for being on this journey of planning a loving legacy. I have so much admiration and respect for you.

Dealing with all of this legal paperwork isn't simple, but it is an essential responsibility that will mean so much to the people you love. You are a family hero for taking this on!

Once you have all your paperwork completed and notarized, I encourage you to plan a special dinner with your family to share the good news with them and tell them how much you love them.

To help a little with the "talking stuff," I've got some playful resources for you. It can be good to bring a little lightness or humor into any part of life that challenges us. To that end, part of your celebration can be checking out resources like "The Death Deck" or "Death Over Dinner," both of which lighten things up!

Click here for my "Way to Go Celebration Audio," as well as some easy and playful ways to talk about all of this with people you love. (Hopefully what I share there will make you laugh!)

- Do I think my assets are simple enough that I can use DIY online legal forms or will I hire an estate planning attorney?

- Have I already begun talking about some of these decisions with my loved ones or will I be opening the door in a brand new way?

- Do I want to use any kind of conversation tool like *The Death Deck* or "Five Wishes" with my next of kin? Or do I prefer a simple, straightforward conversation that I initiate?

- How can I make this process feel fulfilling and joyful? How will I keep my focus on the peaceful impact it will have on people I love?

- Have I chosen to use a prepared organizing system like Nokbox or will I create my own filing system using a fireproof box or some other keep-it-all-in-one-place container?

- Do I feel ready to start setting up my filing system now so all of these important legal papers are easy to access?

☑ Section 1 Worksheet: Checklist and Fill In

Personal Information:

Full legal name _____

Date and place of birth _____

Social Security number (or where it can be located) _____

Passport number (if applicable) _____

Driver's license number _____

Contact information (address, phone number, email) _____

_____

Health insurance information _____

Primary care doctor's name and number _____

_____

Estate planning attorney name and number _____

_____

Having your legal documents created, brought together, and (when applicable) notarized can help ensure that your wishes are respected and that your affairs are managed appropriately in the event of serious illness or hospitalization.

Here's a checklist of important legal documents to consider gathering and creating:

Birth and Marriage Certificates:

Birth certificate, Social Security card, marriage certificate, and divorce decree

❏ Birth Certificate (Located _____)

❏ Social Security Card (Located _____)

❏ Marriage Certificate (Located _____)

❏ Divorce Decree (Located _____)

Advance Directive (Living Will):

An advance directive outlines your preferences for medical treatment and end-of life care if you become unable to communicate your wishes. It typically includes instructions regarding life-sustaining treatments, resuscitation, and organ donation. Ask your physician if you need a POLST: Physician Orders for Life-Sustaining Treatment.

❑ Advance Directive (Located _____)

❑ POLST (Located _____)

Last Will and Testament:

A will outlines how you want your assets and belongings to be distributed after your death. It also appoints an executor to manage your estate and names guardians for any minor children, other dependents, and pets.

❑ My estate planning attorney is (name) _____

❑ My will can be found (Located _____)

Health Care Power of Attorney (Health Care Proxy):

A health care power of attorney form appoints someone to make health care decisions on your behalf if you are unable to do so. Choose someone you know and trust who understands your values and with whom you've had conversations about your medical care preferences.

❑ My Health Care Power of Attorney is (name) _____

❑ Health Care Power of Attorney Form (Located _____)

HIPAA Authorization:

This is your signed permission to allow a specified entity, such as a medical services provider, to use or disclose your protected health information.

❑ I have completed a HIPAA Authorization (Located _____)

Durable Power of Attorney:

A durable power of attorney authorizes someone to manage your financial and legal affairs if you become incapacitated. This person can make decisions related to banking, investments, property, and other financial matters.

❏ My Durable Power of Attorney is (name) _____

❏ My Durable Power of Attorney Form (Located _____)

Revocable Living Trust:

A revocable living trust allows you to transfer ownership of assets into the trust and designate beneficiaries to receive those assets upon your death. Unlike a will, a trust can help avoid probate and provide privacy for your estate distribution.

❏ I have set up a trust using this attorney (name) _____

❏ My documents can be found here (Located _____)

Legal Business Forms:

❏ Business Continuation (Located _____)

❏ Buy-Sell Agreement (Located _____)

❏ Succession Plan (Located _____)

❏ Operating Agreement (Located _____)

❏ Partnership Agreement (Located _____)

❏ Trust Documents (Located _____)

NOTE: These documents will be covered in later sections of this book:

Funeral and Burial Instructions: Consider documenting your preferences for funeral arrangements, burial or cremation, and other end-of-life arrangements. Share this information with your loved ones and include it as part of your estate planning documents. (See pages 63-68.)

Digital Estate Plan: Consider creating a digital estate plan that outlines how you want your online accounts, digital assets, and social media profiles to be managed after your death. Provide instructions for accessing and managing these accounts, as well as any passwords or login information. (See pages 97-98.)

Financial Institutions and Household Management Instructions: Consider creating documents that clearly point your next of kin to all financial and household accounts and passwords. (See pages 93-96.)

Note: It's important to consult with an experienced attorney who specializes in estate planning to ensure that your legal documents comply with state laws and accurately reflect your wishes. Also, our lives and circumstances change over time. Remember to review and update your documents at least every two to three years to keep them current and relevant to your circumstances.

Care and Comforts During Illness

"I can be changed by what happens to me.
But I refuse to be reduced by it."

—Maya Angelou

We Just Keep Doing Our Best, No Matter What

Some Brief Guidance on This Section

As we travel this journey together, preparing for all kinds of uncertainties the future may hold, I want to start this section with two very important phrases: self-love and self-compassion.

Whatever this moment holds for you, whether you are navigating an illness or not, it is important to offer yourself a big dose of kindness and grace. Take a deep breath as we consider some preparations that will make our current or future health declines a little easier on ourselves and others.

Hopefully you'll read some suggestions and learn some new tools that will ease the path of illness and dying—whether that is around the next bend or many years to come.

Loving Yourself As You Navigate Illness

Plan to Surround Yourself with Lots of Support

In the last section, you completed some essential health-related documents like the Advance Health Care Directive and your General and Durable Power of Attorney for Health Care. Good for you! Those are huge legal steps toward getting things in order.

In this section of the book, we're giving you a moment to reflect on some other kinds of preparations—thinking about some of the choices that may come up down the road.

Because everyone who is reading this book will likely be at different ages and in various stages of health and wellness, you will want to lean into the Resources Directory to learn more about specific areas with which you want to go deeper. (Remember, that directory is at the very end of this book!)

For now, let's just review some types of support that may be available to you when the time comes during which you are navigating illness. Allow yourself to simply swim around in the terms and ideas for now—and take note that when it comes to these health care support issues, you will likely know more about what you want or don't want when you are at the doorway to those decisions.

Learning about the world of illness and dying when we aren't in dire circumstances can allow for a more thoughtful—and perhaps less emotionally charged—understanding of these services and areas of care.

Here's a general list of some of the many kinds of support that you may choose to seek out when you are ill:

- **Family and Friends:** Provide emotional, practical, and social support— perhaps even acting as primary caregivers and advocates for you.

- **Support Groups:** Groups that provide emotional support and discussion of shared experiences for people with similar illnesses or conditions.

- **Home Health Care:** Medical and nonmedical services provided in your home to support ongoing health needs.

- **Spiritual Care:** Emotional and spiritual support provided by chaplains or spiritual advisors. These may be integrated into palliative and hospice care.

- **Mental Health Support:** Counseling and therapy services to help people manage the emotional challenges of illness.
- **Geriatric Care Management:** Coordination of care services for elderly or chronically ill individuals, addressing medical, social, and financial needs.
- **Assisted Living:** Residential facilities providing assistance with daily activities and medical care in a supportive environment.
- **Palliative Care:** A multidisciplinary team of specialists focuses on providing relief from the symptoms and stress of a serious illness, enhancing quality of life.
- **Hospice:** Specialized care for those nearing the end of life, emphasizing comfort and support rather than looking for further cures or treatment.
- **End-of-Life Doulas:** Nonmedical professionals offering emotional, spiritual, and practical support to individuals and families during the dying process.
- **Long-Term Care Facilities:** Nursing homes or skilled nursing facilities offering ongoing medical care and assistance with daily living.
- **Social Services:** Assistance with navigating health care systems, accessing benefits, and coordinating care, often provided by social workers.
- **Complementary and Alternative Medicine (CAM):** Therapies like acupuncture, massage, and herbal treatments used alongside conventional medical care.
- **Pet Therapy:** Interaction with animals to provide emotional support, reduce stress, and encourage physical activity, improving overall well-being.

On the worksheet at the end of this section, you can list which of these support systems appeal to you. And perhaps there are others you want to add that I didn't list?

Thinking a little about these options at this point in your life will help you make more informed decisions about your care preferences and treatments down the road.

EXPERT TIP:
Use Free Resources for Added Support During Illness

"For anyone who is ill or who has suffered a loss or trauma, look up supportnow. org. This free resource will help you and your family organize meal trains and other necessary tasks that can be overwhelming during difficult times."

—Jo-Anne Haun, cofounder of the Death Doula Network of BC

Consider This: You Don't Have to Go Through Illness Alone, Even If You Don't Have a Partner or Children

Many people aren't aware that there are caring professionals whose mission in life is to support their fellow human beings on the journey through illness and the end of life. These professionals, known as end-of-life doulas or death doulas, are generally deeply compassionate people who are also well-versed in all the legalities and emotional hurdles you will encounter.

This is a good option for anyone, but especially for people who may not have a partner, children, or other family to care for them.

Sara Zeff Geber, author of *Essential Retirement Planning for Solo Agers*, says, "I'm a big fan of engaging a death doula. I think it's a great option for solo agers who may not have a loving escort as they leave this world. A death doula can be by their side until the very end."

To learn more about this support, click the QR code.

Learn more about the wide range of services and support an end-of-life doula can offer you. It may be just the guiding hand that you need.

☀ EXPERT TIP:

Imagine New Possibilities For Yourself
and Your Living Situation

"I've seen so many cases of a person who wants to age in place, and I think it can be a wonderful idea. And yet, it's a rare exception when I see somebody who's stayed in their longtime home who is healthy, connected, and living their life to their fullest.

Usually, they've shrunk into just one room and the kitchen and they're living a lonely life filled with fear and limitations. It's so sad. They can't even go up the stairs anymore, and they don't even know what's going on up there in those rooms. There could be raccoons living upstairs. I mean, I've seen it—there *have been* raccoons upstairs!

Whereas, there might be somebody else who did their planning far in advance, moved into assisted living, and now they have a community right there for them. Now, all of a sudden they're leading the book club, tending a community garden, and sharing dinners with others."

—Cynthia Cummins, San Francisco realtor and podcast host

Preparing Comforts in Advance, Just in Case

Some Extra Ways to Be Kind to Yourself

You know how people create go bags in case there's an emergency and they have to evacuate? Well, I've been compiling my own go bag as a way to have a collection of comforts when I'm gravely ill—whether at home, in the hospital, or in hospice.

I started by creating a playlist of favorite music from all throughout my life. Many of the songs have special memories attached, so they are an auditory walk down memory lane. My audio playlist also includes talks by my spiritual teacher as well as recordings of friends and family. (I often take snippets of audio to capture joyful moments with people. Listening to them is an instant lift!)

I also printed out a small collection of my very favorite photos of family and friends. That way, no matter what, I will be surrounded by faces of people I love.

Other things in my bag include a couple handmade scarves, a cozy throw my sister gave me years ago, four favorite books, and a note to myself listing some items of clothing that are especially comfy and make me feel good. That list also requests that my Buddhist rosary and a couple pieces of special jewelry be included. (I'll add those in at the last minute! Or someone can do that for me.)

It feels good to send this love out to my future self! Whenever that day comes, I know this go bag will make me feel soothed and comforted. What will you put in your go bag? You can start by making a written list. Then, find a backpack or carry bag you love and start to fill it with love and care.

Some categories of things to put in your go bag:

- Favorite books or passages that people could read to you
- Spiritual texts, poems, or quotes
- Letters or cards from people you love
- Memorabilia items that make you smile

- Music that soothes or uplifts

- A list of foods you love

- Your favorite tea bags

- A list of favorite movies or TV shows to watch

- Photos of people you love

- Comfy sweaters and quilts

- A lavender eye mask

- Sweet or pleasing-smelling lotions and creams

🔍 USEFUL TOOLS:

Create a "Care & Comforts" Playlist Now—Make It Easy

Do you have a digital place where you currently collect and save music? Whether you use an app like Spotify, Pandora, or iTunes, or manage your music in desktop folders, you can make the process of creating your "Care & Comforts" audio playlist an easy effort that you begin right away.

I bet as you are reading this, you could pause and think about three songs that have meaning to you. They might be go-to songs for whenever you need a pick-me-up, or they might have special memories attached. Your favorite high school dance tune? Your wedding dance song? Music you always listen to while doing yoga or walking in nature?

Start with those three. Put them together wherever you collect music, and give that playlist a name that will help spark you to keep adding to it.

Then, whenever another memorable song pops into your head, add it to your list. I started doing this four years ago, and I now have more than two hundred songs on my playlist!

Loving Others As You Navigate Illness

Taking Time to Review Your Legal Documents

In the last section, we talked about how important it is to have conversations with the people you love about all of your plans and preparations.

You have already shared with them where documents are stored, why you made some of the choices you did, and what sorts of questions were still outstanding.

When you fall ill, that is a good time to review all of those documents and open up conversations around end-of-life care. You can use the "Support List" we provided on page 57 a place to start those additional conversations about what you want and don't want.

Savoring In-Person Time with Friends and Family

It's not uncommon for someone who is ill to think that they're protecting someone by not sharing the gravity of their illness, when it might actually be better to include them.

I think this is related to the bigger theme of death and dying. A lot of people think, "Oh, I don't want to bring this up with people I love. I don't want to upset them by talking about illness or death." But actually, this isn't protecting them—it is excluding them from a special kind of intimacy and connection.

There's no right or wrong, no black or white answer. Let's just take some time to think about the various aspects of this so you can make the best decisions for yourself and your loved ones if the time comes when you are faced with a serious illness.

A fellow life coach, Shawn Buttner, shared this story with me recently:

> Some years ago, my brother and I were celebrating his thirtieth birthday on Catalina Island with our wives. The last day we were there, we called home to say hi to our folks. During that call, my mom said, "Oh, tomorrow I'm going in for heart surgery." When we exclaimed about this and asked why she didn't tell us earlier, she said, "I didn't want to burden you with this while you were having fun." I know that she wanted to somehow protect us from the feelings, but it backfired. We wanted to be there. We would have made plans to be there well in advance.

I've heard from other people that they were shut out of someone's life completely when that person became ill. It may not have been a conscious decision, but it left a lasting heartbreak.

If we bring intention, thoughtfulness, and love for our family into the dying process, it's going to make a difference—just like it does when we're alive.

One of my friends (who asked not to be named because of the sensitivity of her story) told me this:

> When my father-in-law was ill, we had no engagement with him at all. We didn't get to see him—or even talk to him—in his last months, even though we lived just minutes away. It was so distressing. My husband's family kind of fell apart and is still struggling with that experience many years later. It left a painful chasm and tainted our memories of my father-in-law. I don't think my husband's dad understood at the time that this would be his legacy. Otherwise, I'm sure he would have handled it differently.

I understand that when people are ill and experiencing physical suffering, many of us shut down and want privacy. However, it feels important to consider the people being left behind and what happens when they don't get a chance to see you and tell you what is in their hearts.

Contrast that last story with this one that my friend (and fellow life coach) Michelle Huljev told me:

> When my grandmother passed away in her nineties, everyone in my family got a chance to spend a short bit of time with her one-on-one. My mom and aunts kindly told me, "This is your time with Grandma to tell her whatever you want—anything important you want her to know." They even said, "It's okay if you cry. Grandma will understand."
>
> I feel so emotional just talking about it because it was so intentional and beautiful. I'm so grateful I got that time to hold her hand, express my love to her, and share with her how inspirational she'd been in my life. It was very important to me.

Again, I'm not trying to make anyone right or wrong in their decisions. However, like so many other aspects of legacy planning, how we choose to interact—or not—during an illness or the dying process can have a tremendous impact on our loved ones.

Just like with books or movies, our final chapter could be the one that lingers in people's minds. Let's do whatever we can to provide a loving last impression.

Setting Intentions Now for Who You Want to Be

One of my favorite coaching tools is a simple one that I learned from my mentor, high performance coach Brendon Burchard. When I was certified by Brendon, I learned one of the most valuable tools ever: Choose words that describe how and who we want to be in specific situations.

For instance, if I am traveling to see my mom, I will think in advance, "loving," "generous," and "playful." Those words become a mantra as I'm traveling and when I am with my mom. They remind me to live into them and be the kind of person I most want to be around her.

I suggest we do this for all of our meetings with people, the events we attend, and the seasons of our lives!

As you look ahead to a time in your life when you may not be as healthy or mobile as you are now, what three words describe how you want to be? If we don't think of this in advance, we might unintentionally be living out words like "exhausted," "crabby," and "complaining."

Of course, there's nothing wrong with having any of those feelings or expressing them! That is healthy! However, this is a book about our legacy, and as my Zen teacher Cheri Huber says, "How you do anything is how you do everything." Can we *choose* how we want to be with illness and challenges?

Can we decide that we want our legacy to be one of love and humor and care—even during the most difficult situations?

Illness and dying are not separate chapters of our lives! We are *alive*—every step of the way until we aren't. If we start being more intentional now, we are sure to carry that with us into the next chapter.

⚙️ EXPERT TIP:

You Can Choose to Normalize Illness

"There's a great power to keeping up your routine, to not stopping everything, even when you're ill and not able to do things as well as you could before.

Some people have suggested that because I am going to die soon, I should give up my work or my service to the church. They think I should spend every minute of every day with my children, that I should hold them physically and emotionally close—in a kind of bubble.

However, I've noticed my children respond well when I'm normal. If I stay at home crying and say, 'Why don't we all give up and stay home crying?' they wouldn't feel like they could keep going with their own lives—their university studies, relationships, travel, and passions.

If I go to work, they feel they can keep going, too. Instead of drowning in my sorrow and pity, they are achieving things. Their lives are continuing to move forward. My courage to do normal things has allowed my children to fly. And I know that when the difficult moment comes that I'm no longer here, their bravery will already be refined. They're learning courage right now.

And we are all learning that somehow, even while carrying all this crap, all this heavy stuff, we have to find a way to live life in a joyful way now."

—Sam Bridgstock (excerpt from *The Greg McKeown Podcast*)

Consider This: Hold a Celebration of Life Now While You Can Enjoy It

If you read Mitch Albom's book *Tuesdays with Morrie*, you may remember that the main character, Morrie Schwartz, holds a "living funeral," or a celebration of life, in which he gets to hear all the wonderful things his friends and family would say at his funeral. He got to hear them while he was alive.

That book and the Death Positive Movement have popularized this idea. When my spiritual teacher turned sixty, our community got to participate in one for her, and it was so beautiful. I still feel the great peacefulness inside of me knowing that I got to express how much she has shaped and transformed my life.

As you're reading this, consider whether a celebration of life might be right for you. In addition to hearing all the beautiful things people have to say about you, you can also use that time with people you love to let them choose items of yours that they would like to have. You get to see the joy on their faces as they receive special gifts that will always remind them of you!

I always remember a beautiful story from my dear friend Suki Haseman about this idea:

> My friend, Anne, had a terminal illness and planned for medical aid in dying. She decided to throw a going-away party for herself and invite all her friends. We had a wonderful potluck, and then we danced, told stories, and wished her well on her next journey.
>
> When you first arrived at the party, Anne had two friends at the door who gave you a name tag and a number. You didn't know what the number was for at first. Later, when your number came up, you could go out to the garage and choose four items from the ones that Anne had put out for people to take. Some of them were personal, but others were just things she didn't want to go to landfill or Goodwill—things we could use and think of her when we did.
>
> There was so much love in that house! It wasn't heavy or depressing. It was all light and love. I remember feelings like it was such a beautiful way to leave this planet.

Consider This: There Could Be a Gift Hidden Here Somewhere!

While I was working on this book, I reached out to someone who had been my therapist many, many years ago, when I was a young woman. He's retired now and has been going through some health challenges. Because he was trained as a psychologist and has also studied Buddhism, I knew he would have some sage wisdom about illness and dying.

Here's what psychologist Douglas Anderson had to say about an unexpected gift of his illness:

> It may sound funny or strange for me to say this, but I feel like this is a gift that my body is going through so much. If I listed all the things I'm dealing with—some of which are life-threatening—it's amazing.
>
> You know that joke about old people getting together and all they talk about is, "Did you go to the doctor again today?" It's true! There are times when we're just rambling on about our illnesses and our bodies changing, or you could say, slowly dying. Yes, my body is breaking down. But that's part of the wake-up. That's why it is a gift.

What Douglas said really struck me: "Breaking down and waking up." When we think about it, hasn't that been a truth that runs through our whole lives? The times we've cracked up or been broken down have often brought us surprising gifts of wisdom, compassion, and openness down the road. We don't ever want to face scary stuff. But haven't we found our way through every other scary thing we've ever faced? And hasn't it usually helped us learn more about ourselves or see more deeply? It's been a gift; or there has been some gift in it.

I'm hoping to bring this philosophy into my own aging and breaking down of the body.

Listen to a beautiful podcast episode in which these decades-long friends are in conversation about terminal illness and the challenges and wisdom it can bring.

? Section 2 Worksheet: Guiding Questions

- Have I reviewed my Health Care Directive and talked to my friends and family about the details again?

- Do I like the idea of putting together a Care and Comforts go bag for myself to have if I need to go to the hospital, hospice, or somewhere else when ill?

- Do I know a little more about what kinds of support will be available and what I might want to avail myself of when the time comes?

- Have I looked at the Resource Directory in the back of the book to see if I want to learn more about support that is available?

- Am I considering talking to any end-of-life doulas just to get a sense of what they do and how they could support me even before I become ill?

☑ Section 2 Worksheet: Checklist and Fill In

Legal Health Forms

Just a reminder that I have completed my Advance Health Care Directive.

You can find it here:_____

A few reminders about conversations that we've had (or that I'd hoped we would have!) to clarify my decisions so you don't have to wonder, worry, or stress:

_____

_____

_____

_____

_____

_____

_____

My general primary care physician is _____

Their contact information: _____

Other doctors and their contact information: _____

_____

_____

_____

_____

_____

_____

Gathering Support Around Me

In the list below of all kinds of support that are possible when I become ill, I've circled ones that I think I'd like to explore.

- Family and Friends

- Palliative Care

- Hospice

- Assisted Living

- End-of-Life Doulas

- Home Health Care

- Caregiver Support

- Geriatric Care Management

- Spiritual Care

- Mental Health Support

- Respite Care

- Long-Term Care Facilities

- Support Groups

- Advance Care Planning

- Rehabilitation Services

- Social Services

- Complementary and Alternative Medicine (CAM)

- Pet Therapy

Additional Care and Comforts: Go Bag

❏ I have a go bag for Care and Comforts. You can find it here _____

There is a list in that bag of extra things to add. Here's what they are and where you will find them. Would you please add these things to the bag if I am unable to do so?

1. _____

Found here _____

2. _____

Found here _____

3. _____

Found here _____

4. _____

Found here _____

5. _____

Found here _____

Additional Care and Comforts: Soothing Music Playlist

❏ I have a playlist of some music and/or audio snippets from people I love. Here's where that can be found on my phone, on a flash drive, or on my computer. I also have headphones. Could you please bring this for me?

My playlist is called _____

Playlist is located here _____

Headphones are located here _____

When I'm Gone: First Things First

"What the caterpillar calls the end of the
world, the master calls a butterfly."
—Richard Bach

This Is Where Your Hard Work Eases the Path

Right now, you are reading this book. You are breathing. You are alive. You are filled with good intentions. You are a wonderful and caring person who loves people and who is willing to put in time and effort to make their lives easier and better on some future date.

I know for most of us it is really hard to imagine that there will be a moment in time when we've transitioned from being a soul in a body to whatever comes next. It is hard to imagine that one day we will no longer wake up and walk around on this planet.

In this section, more than any other in the book, I'm asking you to try it on. Take a deep breath, maybe put a hand on your heart, and imagine the first few moments after you take your very last breath.

It can feel tender to think of your loved ones you will leave behind and to know how sad they will be. However, I also want you to think about the legacy of love you are leaving. I want you to acknowledge that all of these plans you are putting into place are going to give your friends and family great solace in the midst of their grief.

Additionally, it can be really helpful to get in touch with what your spiritual or religious beliefs are about what happens after we die. We aren't going to explore that together because it is a huge topic that has been plumbed in countless books. It is deeply personal and can often shift and change as we age.

We all have different beliefs about that "what comes next" part. I honor and respect whatever your beliefs are about what happens after we die. The reason I ask you to bring those beliefs to the surface right now is that you will be making decisions about what you'd like done to your physical body after you die. You'll be thinking about ritual, ceremony, and celebrations of your life. You'll be guiding your next of kin on who they should contact and how they will handle things like your obituary.

These are not easy things to think about. However, if we ground them in our bigger beliefs about life, that can be helpful. It can allow us to move through this decision-making with some guideposts and with the knowledge that we are taking care of ourselves in the best way we know how—with honesty, compassion, and love.

A Loving Note to Friends or Family Who Are Reading This After You've Passed

This is the hardest part of being human. What you are going through right now is deeply painful, and I encourage you to be as gentle, patient, and kind with yourself and those around you as possible.

No one escapes grief, but that doesn't make it any more bearable. What makes it bearable is when we lean on others for support and when we summon up the best of ourselves as we navigate it.

I've included some of my favorite resources on grief in the back of this book. I hope you will take a look and use some of them to bring you understanding and a bit of relief.

There is no right or wrong way to go through grief. Your sister may express it in an entirely different way than your brother, aunt, or uncle. Some people go into shock. Some people withdraw.

Please try to be as compassionate as possible with what your process is. And offer as much as you can of that understanding and love to others, as well.

One important thing to remember is that grief will run its course in its own time and way. In the first days and weeks, there are so many logistics to handle. Your loved one has done everything they can to try to make this process simple and straightforward for you. They've worked hard to leave you the gift of having their plans in order.

Carry their love in your heart as you carry out their wishes.

Go slowly. Be gentle. One moment at a time.

My friend Shawn Buttner, who is also a high performance coach, gives this helpful guidance as he shares how he navigates grief:

> I view death like, "The show must go on." You still have to cook dinner; you still have to take care of stuff. It's like eating an emotional elephant. You know—one bite at a time. That elephant always follows me around, but it's a little bit smaller and a little bit less intense as time goes on.

When I heard him say this, I remembered an old Zen saying: "Chop wood; carry water." As you are navigating the first hours and days following your loved one's death, try to keep your focus grounded in each moment. Make every activity a practice of being present as much as possible. That will help you stay solid in yourself and not fall into confusion or stress.

At the end of this section is a worksheet your loved one has filled out. It is a checklist for you of the most important things to do following their death.

You don't have to do everything at once. Your loved one has a whole plan. The steps from this section of the book will be the first things you do. Don't worry about other things that don't need to happen right away. You will be guided to those other things in the sections ahead.

"Chop wood; carry water" means you are giving yourself permission to handle one thing at a time.

Please know that your family or friend has written out these instructions with as much awareness, thoughtfulness, and care as possible in order to make these steps go smoothly for you. Carry their love in your heart as you embark on each one.

Taking Time to Plan Out These Three Things Will Make All the Difference for Your Loved Ones

1. Instructions on My Remains

You may already have a sense of the plans you would like for your body after you pass away. Many religions, cultures, or family preferences will dictate this choice for you. However, the world has been changing greatly over the last couple decades, and people have many more options now than ever before.

If you do not make this decision based on your religion or culture, you may look at financial or ecological considerations.

I know for myself, when I first made my end-of-life plans five years ago, I noted that I wanted to be buried in a biodegradable "mushroom suit." I liked the ecological nature of it. However, just two months ago, I changed my directive and filled out the form to have my body donated to UCSF here in San Francisco (where I live) to help further medical research.

I'll tell you why. Working on this book has prompted me to have conversations with my son and my two nieces, who are my closest family members of the next generation. As it turns out, none of them felt that it would be important to have a burial plot or memorial spot to visit. All three felt that if they wanted to feel close to me, they would partake in something I loved—go to a Zumba class, have a piece of berry pie, walk in the botanical gardens, or look through family photos.

When I learned that from our conversations, I realized that I would feel really good about donating my body to science. And you know what else? It doesn't cost anything. The "mushroom burial suit" would cost around $1,500–$2,000, and then there would be the actual burial costs as well. That would have added at least another $1,000–$3,000. Why spend upwards of $5,000 and take up burial space if no one coming after me would even care about such a thing?

I decided I'd rather spend that money now on traveling with my nieces and son and creating memories that will live on in them!

My experience is a good reminder of why it is so helpful to talk to those we leave behind. You may be surprised by what they do or don't care about!

As with all of the other decisions you make for yourself, remember that there is no right or wrong! This is about aligning with what matters most to you and what values are key. Your first decision is based on the three main options:

- **Burial:** The body is interred in the ground, usually in a cemetery, with a casket and a headstone. Alternative options include an in-ground green casket or mushroom suit or above-ground interment in a mausoleum or crypt. (Cremated remains can also be buried.)

- **Cremation:** The body is reduced to ashes via a heat or water process. Cremains (cremated remains) can be kept in an urn, buried in a cemetery plot, buried at sea, buried with a tree or tree pod, turned into jewelry, kept in a columbarium, or scattered in a garden, forest, ocean, or the air.

- **Donation to Science:** The body is donated to medical schools or research institutions for educational and scientific purposes, often followed by cremation.

In general, in terms of finances, the categories above are listed in order of most expensive to least expensive. (Although, of course, there are always exceptions, and it depends on which additional services are requested.)

Within each of those main categories, there are many specific choices to be made. Don't let this overwhelm you! I've created a list of guiding questions for you on page 71. There are many professionals whose job it is to help you make these choices based on your values, your budget, and your family's wishes.

Do the best you can when making these decisions and know that you can always update or change your choices.

If you make a decision to prepay—which can be a very economical route to take because most services will increase in price as time goes by—then trust your decision and know that you did your best to select what feels right for you. As with almost all decisions in our lives, we must trust ourselves and affirm that we did our very best when weighing the options.

Consider This: Making Visits Easy for Those You Leave Behind

I want to encourage you to keep returning to imagining how your decisions will impact the people you love. It is easy to want to rush through this process and choose what feels best to us. However, remember that we are creating our loving legacy, right now, with every decision we make.

For instance, one of my friends told me that her parents have planned for and paid for cremation, which is a big gift to her and her sisters; this way, they know for sure what will happen and what their parents want. However, their parents have also paid for having their cremains interred in a columbarium in South Carolina, where they currently reside.

None of the daughters live anywhere close to that state. In fact, the town where the columbarium is located is very complicated to get to from where they live. "I can't imagine that I will ever travel all of that distance to a place where I don't know anyone, simply to visit their ashes," my friend said.

Another friend had a very different experience. She told me that her mom had opted to have her ashes scattered in the ocean through the Neptune Society. "What I love about that is that anytime I am near the ocean—no matter where it is in the world—I feel like I am visiting my mom."

Those are just two simple examples of why talking to our next of kin can have a huge impact on the plans we make right now.

2. Instructions on Funeral, Memorial, or Celebration Services

Your next key decision to make has to do with whether you would like to have any kind of service or event so that loved ones can have a chance to gather together.

Before you make a hasty yes-or-no decision about this, I encourage you (yet again!) to have a heart-to-heart talk with your closest friends and family members.

Many people want to be humble, and so they'll say, "No funeral or service is necessary." But remember Shawn's story about his mom being ill and not wanting to "bother" her children with it? This is kind of the same thing! The people you love may *want* to honor you. In most cases, families will benefit greatly from a gathering of some kind.

It can be important for the bereaved to have the kind of closure that such a service or event can provide. For many people, connecting with others who love you will be a lifeline during such deep sadness and grief. A service of some kind offers permission to grieve and to express that grief out loud.

Please don't decide this for them; ask them.

Then, once you've got a decision about whether or not to have a service, your next decision is based on the three main options:

- **Funeral:** Typically, funerals are traditional events held shortly after death, where the body or ashes may be present. Funerals often include religious or cultural rites and traditional readings of appropriate passages.

- **Memorial:** These may be less traditional events, and they are usually held without the body present, thus the timing can be more flexible—even weeks or months after the death.

- **Celebration of Life:** These are informal events which usually focus more on the joyful elements of someone's life instead of on grief and loss.

Just like with the previous decision about the body, within each of these main categories, there are also many specific choices to be made. I'm here with you. Don't worry. You'll find my list of guiding questions for you on page 71. And as previously noted, there are also many professionals whose job is to help you make these choices based on your values, your budget, and your family's wishes.

You may want to pop over to those guiding questions now and let yourself think about them, without pressure. Sometimes when we allow ourselves to relax, our instincts and intuition kick in and things may become obvious to us.

-ॉ- EXPERT TIP:

Honor the Wishes of Your Friends and Family

"I was traveling abroad when I got an email that my dad had been diagnosed with terminal cancer, so I came home early. He passed six weeks later, and I was grateful to have been there.

My dad did not want a service, and we honored that. It's one of the few regrets I have, because the service wasn't for him, it was for us.

I believe it is important to honor a person's wishes—whether they want to be cremated, have their ashes spread, or something else—but I believe the service and the way we mourn are for the survivors, not for the deceased.

Survivors need to acknowledge that the person we love is no longer with us. We need to be able to come together as a community and share sad and funny stories. For those who can't cry, watching someone else cry can trigger our mirror neurons and allow us to experience that catharsis as well."

—Dr. Morgan Oaks, chiropractor, high performance coach, and transformational speaker

---

Consider This: Your Values Are Important—and So Are Theirs!

When you review the guiding questions on pages 71-74, you will likely notice that many of them have to do with who you are and what matters to you. It is important to make these decisions from a place of love and respect for oneself and one's own values. It is also important to listen to what matters to our loved ones.

I met a new friend, Dianne Myhre, at a luncheon held by the Neptune Society where the organization was explaining all about their cremation services. Dianne and her husband, a friendly couple in their sixties, were finishing up their end-of-life plans and had decided to attend that luncheon to find out about cremation costs.

My ears perked up when Dianne told me they already knew what they wanted to do with the cremains and that they'd already paid for it. They had signed on with a company called Better Place Forests that would mix their ashes with redwood tree roots in a beautiful California forest. It sounded so peaceful!

Here's what Dianne said:

> My husband and I didn't want a traditional burial, so we were happy to find a memorial forest where your ashes can be mixed with the roots of a tree, becoming part of it. The company we chose also mixes in wildflower seeds, making it a beautiful place for descendants to visit. We chose a redwood tree in Point Arena, California, where he and I, along with three of our pets, will rest.
>
> The part that mattered to us was becoming part of the forest. The memorial or celebration will be up to my husband's daughter. We've set aside money for it, but she can plan whatever she wants. The forest has an outdoor structure like a chapel where you can see the ocean, so if she wants a religious ceremony, she can have it there. The company will set up chairs overlooking the ocean for a small gathering, or visitors can walk the premises, exploring the hills, forest, wildflowers, and creek.
>
> Whatever she chooses is fine with me. If people want to dance around the tree, do pagan rites, or have a sob fest, it's up to them. What happens at the site is not really for those who have passed away; it's for everyone who is grieving.

I like that she separated out what was important to her and her husband and what she wanted his daughter to decide.

Consider This: Money Matters

When I was at that same Neptune Society lunch where I met Dianne, I also had the chance to talk to others about end-of-life plans. One couple told a horror story about a relative of theirs who had passed away. Thankfully, that person had detailed everything they wanted to happen with their body and with the funeral service and burial. They listed all of the details, including what kind of casket, which funeral home, which cemetery, what kind of engraved headstone, and so forth.

What that person hadn't done was to pay for all of those wishes or to earmark funds for it. All told, the family spent more than $25,000 to carry out what their loved one had outlined.

You can imagine how distressing that situation could be! On one hand, we would be grieving and would want to do the right thing for the person we love who has passed away.

On the other hand, we'd have to wonder whether that person had any idea how expensive those plans were and whether they were really that important to them.

We've talked a lot in this book about the emotional peace you are leaving behind with your end-of-life plans. Hopefully, you can also appreciate that you are leaving financial peace to those who survive you as well. I doubt that any of us want to unintentionally saddle our family or friends with financial hardship or debt because they would feel guilty otherwise.

EXPERT TIP:

Plan Something Truly Personal for the Service That Will Feel Like *You*!

"I've got a folder with all the ideas of things I'd want at my memorial or life celebration. I definitely want there to be bubbles. I love bubbles! Also, people know me for my colorful ties—I have more than 100 of them!— so I've asked that there be a round table at the end of the event, with all the ties laid out in a circle so everyone can take one as they leave.

I asked my daughter's friend, who did an incredible job of planning her mother's memorial celebration, if she would do mine. She said yes, and I've arranged for payment for her work.

For the celebration, I've included lists of the songs I want, whom I'd like to speak, and the kind of food I want—all Jewish food—and Klezmer music when people come in and leave. I've just started writing down my wishes in this folder, and I keep adding to it whenever I think of something else.

I encourage everyone to do this so your memorial or life celebration feels more personal."

—Allen Klein, author and speaker

3. Instructions on Who to Contact—Plus Notes on Children, Pets, and Dependents

The third most important thing you can do for your loved ones to help them on the day you pass away is to leave them a list of important contacts, including family members, friends, and professionals who should be notified of your passing.

This will be fairly easy and straightforward for you to compile, but can you imagine what it would be like for them if you don't? Most of us have smartphones with contact lists filled with dozens, if not hundreds, of names with phone numbers and/or emails. It is easy enough for us to know that Bill Jones was someone we met at a conference five years ago and with whom we quickly lost touch, and that Jean Smith is a dear friend who lives in England who no one else in our life knows, but who matters greatly.

It is also fairly easy for us to group our friends and acquaintances in a way that would make creating phone trees quite simple. We can list the five high school friends we keep in touch with and designate one of them as the coordinator who will call the others. We can give the name and contact for our boss at work and count on that person to let the whole staff know.

Use the worksheet in the back of this book to write in the names of contacts and the main coordinators of phone tree groups. Or if you have a large community, you will likely want to type these out and designate on the worksheet in this book where your next of kin can find that printed or digital list. Your next of kin need to be able to immediately find out who you have named as guardian for any minor children or other dependents. This is also incredibly important for our animal companions.

Imagine again those first few hours after you have passed. What if your family is scrambling to find the documents telling them who should look after your children and pets? What if your family members don't even know those documents exist?

Now, think about how calming it will feel for them to check the worksheet at the back of this book and see that all of this information is typed up and filed away where they can easily access it.

See worksheet on pages 75-90.

Celebrate These Loving Decisions

I'm so incredibly proud of you! This was a big set of decisions, and I know it required you to dig deep inside of yourself to find what matters. It also asked you to have some tough conversations with the people you love.

No one wants to think about a time when we aren't here anymore or when we will lose people we love. But the three big areas of planning that you just completed will bring more peace of mind to your family and friends than you can even imagine right now.

The gift you've just given them is clear, easy-to-follow instructions that will relieve them of having to scramble to find answers for things or being left to argue amongst themselves. You've given them a gift with "Chop wood; carry water" instead of a tornado of confusion and swirls of uncertainty on what direction to go. You have given them time and space to do what is truly most important in the hours and days after you die—to be with their grief and to share that grief with others without undue drama or stress.

How will you celebrate these three big steps you just took? I've got you! Click the QR code below to find out more!

You are *amazing*! Click here to celebrate
completing these three big sets of instructions!

Questions to Ask Myself Regarding My Remains

- Are there religious or cultural dictates about how one's body is cared for after death?

- Are there financial considerations that affect this choice?

- Will I be paying for these services in advance to save my loved ones the expense and trouble?

- If I am asking my loved ones to pay for these services, are there funds earmarked for this in my bank account or elsewhere so they do not have to carry the financial burden?

- Are there environmental values that I want to align with when making this decision?

- Have I discussed these matters with my closest relatives, the ones whom these decisions will most impact?

- If I have chosen burial, have I also researched and selected the type of casket or pine box, burial plot, and headstone? Do I want an eco-burial or a more traditional burial? Have I considered if I want a viewing with an open casket? Have I thought about embalming (which will likely be required if I want an open casket viewing)? Have I spoken with a funeral home, cemetery coordinator, green burial director, end-of-life doula, or estate planner about the many choices associated with burial?

- If I have chosen cremation, have I also researched and selected whether I want the cremains to be buried in a cemetery (interment), kept in a columbarium, scattered someplace special, placed in an urn, planted with a tree, turned into a keepsake item, or incorporated into a coral reef? Have I spoken with a cremation provider, funeral home, cemetery coordinator, green burial director, end-of-life doula, or estate planner about the many choices associated with cremation?

- If I have chosen to have part or all of my body donated to science, have I contacted the medical school, research institution, or body donation program to which I intend to make this donation? Have I completed their forms? If I am donating only part of my body, have I discussed with that organization what happens to the remains?

Questions to Ask Myself About a Funeral, Memorial or Celebration of Life

- Have I talked to my closest family and friends to see if it is important to them that there be a service or event of some kind?

- If I have made the decision not to plan a service, is it okay with me if my loved ones choose to do what feels best to them in the absence of plans? Have I discussed this with them?

- Are there religious or cultural dictates about the kind of service I will choose?

- Do I want to express any of my values through a specific type of service?

- Will I be paying for expenses relating to these services in advance to save my loved ones the expense and trouble?

- If I am asking my loved ones to pay for these services, are there funds earmarked for this in my bank account or elsewhere so they do not have to carry the financial burden?

- If I have chosen a funeral service, would I want a religious or nonreligious service? Would I want it to take place at a church, a funeral home, a cemetery chapel, or some other venue? Open or closed casket? If I want an open casket viewing, would I want to be dressed in something specific? Does an open casket mean I would choose embalming, which most funeral homes require for open casket services? Would I include viewing hours before the funeral? What type of casket? How expensive or inexpensive of a casket? Do I want flowers or other decorations? Music? Readings? Photos or mementos? Who would I want to deliver the eulogy? Who else would I wish to be speakers or readers at the service? Will there be pallbearers? Who? A printed program? Who do I want to be invited to the funeral? Is transportation needed to the cemetery? Will there be a meal or gathering after the funeral? Would

I suggest charitable donations in lieu of flowers? Or if there will be flowers, would I like them given away or donated after the service? Do I have other special requests, such as releasing butterflies or planting a tree afterward?

- If I have chosen a memorial service, would I want a religious or nonreligious service? Would I want it to take place at a church, funeral home, community center, private residence, outdoor location, or other space? Would there be a printed program? Would I want speeches, readings, music, or some other planned structure? Would there be a memento or photo table? A slideshow? Would there be a candle-lighting ceremony? What are the floral arrangements or decorations? Would there be printed or digital invitations? Who would be invited? Would there be a theme or specific rituals I would like?

- If I have chosen a celebration of life, what venue would best match the tone and my spirit—the outdoors, an art gallery, restaurant, private home, or somewhere else? How would I want elements like the music, program, decorations, rituals, memento table, and program to reflect my personality? Would there be printed or digital invitations, and what elements would be included on those? Who would be invited? Would I suggest any quirky or fun favors or mementos to be given to each guest? Would guests be encouraged to wear specific themed clothing or accessories? What added elements would make this celebration make everyone feel connected to me and my life?

Questions to Ask Myself About Important People to Contact

- Just off the top of my head, who are the ten to twenty most important people in my life? Family, friends, colleagues, and any others who matter should be on this list.

- Do I have children, pets, or other dependents who will need immediate care, attention, and housing when I pass away? Even if I have a spouse or roommates, how can I plan for these dependents if that person or those people were not available?

- Do I have an employer who would need to be contacted right away? Is there a human resources department at my job that could help with logistics?

- What are some groupings of friends or acquaintances for whom I could appoint one person as a contact? For example, such groupings could include a hobby club or a professional organization.

- Do I have ongoing clients who are on my schedule and who would need to be contacted if something were to happen to me?

- What professionals—physicians, end-of-life doula, attorney, financial advisor, and so on—would need to be contacted?

☑ Section 3 Worksheet: Checklist and Fill In

1. INSTRUCTIONS REGARDING MY REMAINS

I have completed the following written instructions:

❏ I have made my final decisions and paid for burial or cremation services.

These documents can be found here _____

❏ I haven't paid for a funeral or cremation; however, my wishes are written out and can be found here _____

Funds for these services can be taken from my bank account. Call _____

❏ I've chosen to donate my body to science. I've filed those forms with _____.

_____

Those forms and the phone number can be found _____

I haven't had a chance to formally document all of my wishes, but here is a quick checklist and some of my thoughts that I hope will be helpful to you in the meantime:

General

❏ I have considered religious or cultural dictates about how the body is cared for after death.

Here is what I have decided: _____

❏ I have evaluated financial considerations regarding this choice.

Here is what I have decided: _____

❏ I have planned to pay for these services in advance to save loved ones the expense and trouble.

Here is what I have decided: _____

❏ I have ensured funds are earmarked in a bank account or elsewhere to cover expenses if I am asking my loved ones to pay for these services.

Here is where to find those funds: _____

❏ I have aligned my decision-making process with environmental values.

Here is what I have decided: _____

❏ I have had conversations with my closest relatives, the ones whom these decisions will most impact.

Here is what I learned is important to them: _____

_____

_____

Burial

❏ I have researched and selected the type of casket or pine box, burial plot, and headstone I would prefer.

Here is what I have decided: _____

❏ I have decided between an eco-burial or a more traditional burial.

Here is what I have decided: _____

❏ I have considered if I want a viewing with an open casket (for which embalming may be required).

Here is what I have decided: _____

❏ I have decided whether or not to opt for embalming.

Here is what I have decided: _____

❏ I have spoken with a funeral home, cemetery coordinator, columbarium director, green burial director, end-of-life doula, or estate planner about burial choices.

Here are some other miscellaneous thoughts about burial as an option:

_____

_____

_____

_____

_____

_____

Cremation

❏ I have researched and selected how the cremains will be handled (buried, scattered, placed in an urn, or something else).

Here is what I have decided: _____

❏ I have consulted with a cremation provider, funeral home, cemetery coordinator, green burial director, end-of-life doula, or estate planner about cremation options.

Here is what I have decided: _____

❏ Here are some other miscellaneous thoughts about cremation as an option and what to do with the cremains:

_____

_____

_____

_____

_____

_____

Donating to Science

❏ I have contacted the medical school, research institution, or body donation program to which I intend to donate my body.

Here is the contact information for them: _____

❏ I have completed the necessary forms for body donation to science.

Find those forms here: _____

❏ If donating only part of my body, I have discussed with the organization what happens to the remains.

Here is what I have decided: _____

Here are some other miscellaneous thoughts about donating my body to science:

_____

_____

2. INSTRUCTIONS ON A FUNERAL, MEMORIAL, OR CELEBRATION OF LIFE SERVICE

Obituary:

❏ I've gathered the information for my obituary.

These documents can be found _____

_____

Funeral services:

I have completed written instructions regarding the following:

❏ I have made my final decisions and paid for event services.

These documents can be found _____

❏ I haven't paid for an event; however, my wishes are written out and can be found here.

_____

Funds for these services can be taken from my bank account. Call _____

_____

I haven't had a chance to formally document all of my wishes, but here is a quick checklist and some of my thoughts that I hope will be helpful to you in the meantime:

I would like a funeral:

Service Type

❏ I have considered whether I want a religious or nonreligious service.

Here is what I have decided: _____

Venue

❏ I have decided where I want the service to take place, at a church, funeral home, cemetery chapel, or another venue.

Here is what I have decided: _____

Casket Preference

❏ I have decided whether I want an open or closed casket.

Here is what I have decided: _____

Clothing

❏ If I have an open casket, I have chosen what I want to be dressed in.

Here is what I have decided: _____

Embalming

❏ I have considered whether I would choose embalming (which is likely to be required for an open casket service).

Here is what I have decided: _____

Viewing Hours

❏ I have decided if I want a viewing to take place hours before the funeral.

Here is what I have decided: _____

Casket Selection

❏ I have chosen the type of casket I want.

Here is what I have decided: _____

Casket Budget

❏ I have determined how expensive or inexpensive the casket should be.

Here is what I have decided: _____

Flowers and Decorations

❏ I have decided if I want flowers or other decorations at the service.

Here is what I have decided: _____

Music

❏ I have considered whether I want music at the service and what kind.

Here is what I have decided: _____

Readings

❏ I have decided if there will be readings, and which ones.

Here is what I have decided: _____

Photos and Mementos

❏ I have decided whether I want photos or mementos displayed at the service.

Here is what I have decided: _____

Eulogy

❏ I have decided who I want to deliver the eulogy.

Here is what I have decided: _____

Other Speakers and Readers

❏ I have chosen any other speakers or readers for the service.

Here is what I have decided: _____

Pallbearers

❏ I have decided if there will be pallbearers and who they will be.

Here is what I have decided: _____

Program

❏ I have considered whether I want a printed program for the service.

Here is what I have decided: _____

Guest List

❏ I have decided who I would like to invite to the funeral.

Here is what I have decided: _____

Transportation

❏ I have considered whether transportation is needed to the cemetery.

Here is what I have decided: _____

Post-Funeral Gathering

❏ I have decided whether there will be a meal or gathering after the funeral.

Here is what I have decided: _____

Charitable Donations

❏ I have decided whether to suggest charitable donations in lieu of flowers, and if donations are suggested, to what charity or charities.

Here is what I have decided: _____

Flowers After the Service

❏ If I have flowers, I have decided if I want them given away or donated after the service.

Here is what I have decided: _____

Special Requests

❏ I have considered any special requests, such as releasing butterflies or planting a tree afterward.

Here is what I have decided: _____

I would like a memorial:

Service Type

❏ I have considered whether I want a religious or nonreligious service.

Here is what I have decided: _____

Venue

❏ I have decided where I want the service to take place, at a church, funeral home, community center, private residence, outdoor location, or another space.

Here is what I have decided: _____

Program

❏ I have considered whether I want a printed program for the service.

Here is what I have decided: _____

Structure

❑ I have decided if there will be speeches, readings, music, or another planned structure.

Here is what I have decided: _____

Memento or Photo Table

❑ I have considered whether I want a memento or photo table at the service.

Here is what I have decided: _____

Slideshow

❑ I have decided whether I want a slideshow at the service.

Here is what I have decided: _____

Candle-Lighting Ceremony

❑ I have considered whether I want a candle-lighting ceremony as part of the service.

Here is what I have decided: _____

Flowers and Decorations

❑ I have decided on the floral arrangements or other decorations for the service.

Here is what I have decided: _____

Invitations

❑ I have decided whether I want printed or digital invitations for the service.

Here is what I have decided: _____

Guest List

❑ I have decided who I would like to invite to the service.

Here is what I have decided: _____

Theme or Rituals

❑ I have considered if there will be a theme or specific rituals I would like to include in the service.

Here is what I have decided: _____

I would like a celebration of life:

Venue Selection

❏ I have considered what venue would best match the tone and my spirit—outdoors, art gallery, restaurant, private home, or something else.

Here is what I have decided: _____

Personal Elements

❏ I have considered how elements like the music, program, decorations, rituals, memento table, and program will reflect my personality.

Here is what I have decided: _____

Invitations

❏ I have decided whether to use printed or digital invitations and what elements would be included on those.

Here is what I have decided: _____

Guest List

❏ I have decided who I would like to invite to the celebration.

Here is what I have decided: _____

Favors or Mementos

❏ I have considered if there will be any quirky or fun favors or mementos to be given to each guest.

Here is what I have decided: _____

Themed Attire

❏ I have considered whether guests will be encouraged to wear specific themed clothing or accessories. Here is what I have decided: _____

Connection Elements

❏ I have thought about what added elements would make this celebration make everyone feel connected to me and my life.

Here is what I have decided: _____

3. INSTRUCTIONS ON ESSENTIAL PEOPLE TO CONTACT

I have written instructions completed and stored elsewhere:

❏ I have completed these contact lists and filed them with my important documents.

These documents can be found _____

I haven't had a chance to formally document all of my wishes, but here is a quick checklist and some of my thoughts that I hope will be helpful to you in the meantime:

Guardianship

❏ **Minor Child—Name:**

Person to notify: _____

Phone number: _____

List of favorite toys, food, or belongings to send with them _____

_____

Medications? _____

_____

❏ **Minor Child—Name:**

Person to notify: _____

Phone number: _____

List of favorite toys, food, or belongings to send with them _____

_____

Medications? _____

_____

❏ **Minor Child—Name:**

Person to notify: _____

Phone number: _____

List of favorite toys, food, or belongings to send with them _____

Medications? _____

_____

❑ **Minor Child—Name:**

Person to notify: _____

Phone number: _____

List of favorite toys, food, or belongings to send with them _____

_____

Medications? _____

_____

❑ **Other Dependent—Name:**

Person to notify: _____

Phone number: _____

List of favorite toys, food, or belongings to send with them _____

_____

Medications? _____

_____

❑ **Animal Companion—Name:**

Person to notify: _____

Phone number: _____

List of favorite toys, food, or belongings to send with them _____

_____

Medications? _____

_____

_____

Family, Friends, Associates to Contact

Phone Tree for You

Fill in the blanks below with the names and phone numbers of the people in your closest circles. Please choose a primary contact for each grouping of friends/family. The primary contact can call anyone in that group of the people who know and love you.

Primary Contact for Closest Family Members

This is the person most likely to be notified first in case of my passing. This person will contact my children, parents, siblings, and aunts and uncles.

(Name) _____

(Phone) _____

Names of people this person will contact:

_____

_____

_____

_____

_____

Primary Contact for Distant Family

This is likely a sibling or an aunt or uncle who will contact my cousins, nieces and nephews, and other extended family members.

(Name) _____

(Phone) _____

Names of people this person will contact:

_____

_____

_____

Primary Contact for Friend Group 1

This is a close friend.

(Name) _____

(Phone) _____

Names of people this person will contact:

_____

_____

_____

_____

Primary Contact for Friend Group 2

This is a close friend.

(Name) _____

(Phone) _____

Names of people this person will contact:

_____

_____

_____

_____

Primary Contact for Friend Group 3

This is a close friend.

(Name) _____

(Phone) _____

Names of people this person will contact:

_____

_____

_____

_____

_____

Primary Contact for My Job

This is my boss or Human Resources Director.

(Name) _____

(Phone) _____

Names of my coworkers this person will contact:

_____

_____

_____

_____

_____

Primary Contact for a Club or Volunteer Organization

This is the leader of a club or organization I am involved with.

(Name) _____

(Phone) _____

Names of other members this person will contact:

_____

_____

_____

Other Essential Contacts

❑ Emergency contacts (family members, friends, neighbors)

_____

_____

_____

_____

❑ Primary care physician and specialists

_____

_____

_____

❑ Attorney or legal representative

_____

❑ Financial advisor or accountant

_____

❑ Insurance agents

_____

_____

_____

❑ Executor of your will or trustee of your trust

_____

❑ Employer or retirement plan administrator

_____

❑ End-of-life doula

_____

❑ Doctor or coroner

_____

❑ Local or state vital records office

_____

❑ Funeral home

_____

❑ Employer

_____

❑ Pension provider

_____

❑ Social Security Administration (If using a funeral home or end-of-life doula, they may notify this agency for you)

_____

Note: In the next section, we list many other contacts like financial institutions, utility companies, insurance providers, and so on. These notifications can wait a few days and don't need to be done immediately.

Matters of Money, Household, and Your Family's Future

"Outer order contributes to inner calm."
—Gretchen Rubin

You Are a Family Superhero for Tackling All of This

Most of us generally feel competent in running our lives, right? We know where the bill drawer is, where we keep our banking records, and how to log into each of our digital accounts. That said, even the best of us can find ourselves scratching our heads, wondering, "Where did I put the statements for my 401k?" or "Shoot, that password doesn't work; how do I log into Facebook?"

If we get a bit tripped up running our own households sometimes, imagine if someone we love had to step in and try to navigate it all. Think about what a mess it might be for someone to try to remember and access all of the various automatic subscriptions: the monthly cat food delivery, the vitamin club, the razor deliveries!

This section is going to help you get your household and finances organized, which will be incredibly useful for your loved ones down the road. And guess what? It will feel super good for you to have all this in order for yourself. Once you complete this section, you will be able to easily access all of your own financial and household information!

These Four Steps Will Offer a Sigh of Relief for You and Your Loved Ones

1. Instructions on My Financial Accounts

In the previous section, *When I'm Gone: First Things First*, you did an amazing job of gathering some of the most immediate essential information for your next of kin.

In this section, we are going to dig a little deeper and complete a list of any other financial and household accounts that our loved ones will need to be able to access, review, and close.

Remember that even though this process may be a bit time-consuming for you, for anyone else it would be nearly impossible. When you are reading through the checklist, you will likely know at a glance whether you have any of the kinds of accounts mentioned on it. Then you can methodically track down the information. (Your loved ones, on the other hand, would have absolutely no idea about any of this without your input!)

We highly encourage you to keep all of this financial and account information in a locked safe. Make sure two trusted people have the key and know where that safe is.

If, like me, you are using the Nokbox or another all-in-one-place box system, then in the folder that is labeled "Financial Accounts," simply include a note that says: "This information is located in my fire safe. Jenny Smith and Robert Jones have access to the keys for that safe." That way, your filing system is still the first go-to place for next of kin and it keeps everything clearly noted and organized.

With this dual system in place, Jenny and Robert can be contacted and they will unlock your private information. (Note: You will likely want to give these keys to the holder of your power of attorney and one other trusted person in your life.)

Here Are Some Categories of Accounts for Which You Will Be Providing Information:

- **Bank Accounts:** These can be personal or business accounts, including checking or savings accounts.

- **Retirement Accounts:** This includes 401(k) or Individual Retirement Accounts (IRAs) and could also include pension accounts and Social Security.

- **Investment Accounts:** For example, brokerage accounts.

- **Education Savings Accounts:** For example, 529 plans.

- **Health-Related Accounts:** These accounts include Health Savings Accounts (HSAs) and Flexible Spending Accounts (FSAs).

- **Credit Accounts:** For example, credit cards or personal loans.

- **Mortgage Accounts:** These include home mortgages or Home Equity Lines of Credit (HELOC).

- **Insurance Accounts:** These include life insurance policies or annuities.

- **Trust and Estate Accounts:** For example, either revocable or irrevocable trusts.

- **Other Financial Accounts:** These include money market accounts, certificates of deposit (CDs), or prepaid debit card accounts.

- **Debts and Liabilities:** Some common types are student loans, auto loans, and personal loans.

- **Safe Deposit Boxes:** These can be bank safe deposit boxes or private ones.

2. Instructions on My Automatic Subscriptions

I remember hearing a story from someone recently who had gone away on a three-month vacation and had forgotten to put a hold on her biweekly vitamin and supplement delivery. The boxes were piling up on her porch. Yikes! That was a sure sign that no one was home, one that could have been an invitation for burglaries. You don't want that to happen to your loved ones after you pass!

As with many of the other planning action steps, I'm certain you will find this one to be helpful to you right now. Most people, once they start digging into their subscriptions, realize that they don't even use all of them. It is a good time to cull and cancel.

Here Are Some Categories of Subscription Accounts for Which You Will Be Providing Information:

- **Meal Kits and Grocery Deliveries:** For example, HelloFresh, Blue Apron, or Misfits Market.

- **Streaming Services:** For example, Netflix, Hulu, or Spotify.

- **Beauty and Grooming:** For example, Ipsy, Birchbox, or Dollar Shave Club.

- **Health and Wellness:** For example, Ritual or GNC Pro Access.

- **Clothing and Accessories:** For example, Stitch Fix, Nuuly, or Menlo Club.

- **Books and Magazines:** For example, Book of the Month or Used Books Monthly.

- **Pet Supplies:** For example, BarkBox or CatLadyBox.

- **Alcohol and Beverages:** For example, Shaker & Spoon Cocktail Club or Trade Coffee.

- **Snacks and Specialty Foods:** For example, MunchPak, Universal Yums, or Fit Snack.

- **Fitness:** For example, MuscleBox or FabFitFun. (Also, consider if you have a gym membership that is automatically renewed.)

Remember, just as with your financial account information, you will likely want to have all of these account names and passwords under lock and key in your safe. Slip a note into the "Subscriptions" folder in your Nokbox or other folder system that lets your loved ones know this list is in the safe.

3. Instructions on My Household Details

I know a lot of these next things might sound obvious to you, but sharing details about your household with your family in case of your death is an important part of planning. Not everyone has the same utilities or household systems. It is such a loving act to spell all of this out.

By providing this information, you ensure that your loved ones can not only manage the running of the household, but also take care of financial obligations like bills, mortgages, and insurance—without facing disruptions or penalties.

This knowledge will help them avoid confusion and unnecessary stress during an already challenging time.

Here Are Just a Few Categories to Think About Regarding Your Household:

- **Utility Services:** These include electricity, gas, water, trash/recycling, and internet/phone services.

- **Home Maintenance:** For example, security systems, HVAC maintenance, pest control, landscaping, and snow removal.

- **Property and Homeowner's Insurance:** These include homeowner's insurance, flood insurance, or other property-related policies.

- **Financial and Legal Documents:** For renters, this would include lease or rental agreements, maintenance records, and security deposit receipts. For homeowners, these documents include mortgage information, property taxes, and homeowners association (HOA) details.

- **Miscellaneous Household Information:** A catch-all category that includes post office box information, service contracts, or warranties on appliances.

⊙ USEFUL TOOLS:

Create a "Household How-To" Video to Save Your Family Headaches

"Imagine if something happened to you today and someone had to step into your house and run it. How would they do it? I've got a simple solution: Get your phone and walk around the house and narrate a video to your next of kin.

Show them where the fire safe is, or how the lights turn on, or where you keep household keys. Let them know, 'You should keep this, it's really valuable,' or 'I'm okay if you let this go.' This is where this is. This is where that is. Hopefully you have your own document filing system all set up for your next of kin and can show them on video where you keep it! Email someone that video for great peace of mind."

—Maria Fraietta, founder and CEO of Nokbox

4. Instructions on My Digital Life

Our digital lives are more complex than ever, with so much valuable information stored on our devices and in online accounts.

You can already see how much overlap there is in the previous categories we've looked at. Almost every aspect of our life seems to have an online account attached to it, right?

From important documents, family history, and photos to everyday communications, a lot of what matters most is now digital.

Taking steps to share access to your digital resources is not only thoughtful, it is essential.

Here Are Just a Few Categories to Think About Regarding Our Digital Assets:

- **Financial Management:** This covers online banking, digital accounts like PayPal, Venmo, or cryptocurrency wallets, investment accounts, and budgeting tools.

- **Social Media:** For example, Facebook, Bluesky, or Instagram.

- **Email and Communication:** For example, Gmail, Outlook, or WhatsApp.

- **Entertainment and Media:** For example, Netflix, Spotify, or Kindle.

- **Shopping and Subscriptions:** This includes Amazon, eBay, and subscription boxes.

- **Personal and Professional Document Storage:** This includes Google Drive, Dropbox, cloud storage subscriptions, or password managers.

- **Health and Wellness:** For example, MyChart, Fitbit, Kaiser, or Zocdoc.

- **Travel and Transportation:** For example, Expedia, Uber, or Airbnb.

- **Home Management:** This includes Google Home, Amazon Alexa, or online utility accounts.

- **Education and Learning:** For example, Coursera, Blackboard, or Khan Academy.

- **Legal and Identity Management:** This includes online storage for wills or login information relating to government portals.

- **Business and Professional Services:** For example, Upwork, Microsoft 365, or Adobe Creative Cloud.

- **Photography and Digital Memories:** For example, Google Photos, Shutterfly, or Flickr.

- **Gaming and Virtual Worlds:** For example, Steam, PlayStation Network, or Xbox Live.

- **Memberships and Rewards Programs:** This includes airline loyalty programs, Costco, or gym memberships.

Consider This: Try Using a Password Manager to Make Things Easy

For the last few years, I've used a password manager called 1Password. I used to forget all of my passwords and would get so confused! And then, when a company would write to tell me that they'd had a security breach and I had to update my password, it would be such a pain.

Password managers are software applications that can securely store and manage passwords and other sensitive information like credit card details. Some of the most popular ones are 1Password, LastPass, Dashlane, Bitwarden, or NordPass. These apps generate strong, unique passwords for different accounts and automatically fill them in when needed. Using one has saved me a thousand times over because I have dozens and dozens of online accounts that I need to access quickly.

However, it wasn't until I started working on this book that I realized how incredibly helpful a password manager can be for our next of kin when we pass away.

Here's what 1Password says, "Our digital life is inextricably intertwined with who we are. Embracing ways to thoughtfully pass on access to the digital resources we use every day will not only be a kindness to our loved ones, but also a core part of our legacy."

My 1Password password—literally *one* password—opens up the vault to all my online passwords. That one password is filed away alongside the notarized will and health care directive in my fire safe. Just like with everything else, I have a note in the "Online Accounts" folder in my Nokbox, which reads: "I use 1Password, and all the passwords can be accessed with this password management application. My son and his dad know that one password. It is also in the fire safe along with the other most valuable documents."

Scan Me

How to Plan Your Digital Legacy

1Password has created a free guide, "How to Plan Your Digital Legacy." In this guide, you'll learn how to get started on your own plan, what to do if you've inherited a digital estate plan from someone else, and even how to transfer crypto after you've passed.

You don't have to use their password manager to get a lot of benefit from this document! Scan the code to check it out!

Consider This: Organizing Your Digital Photo Collection

It's impossible for me to think about my digital life without talking about photos. I literally have more than 154,000 photos and nearly 8,000 videos on my desktop computer. We'll be looking at this a bit more in the next section on *The Art of Decluttering and Memory Keeping Before You're Gone*; however, this big topic deserves a jumpstart right now while you're organizing your digital life.

Your photo/video library is something that your loved ones will definitely want access to, right?

I'm currently in the midst of working on culling my photos so I can create a Dropbox folder or flash drive with a curated collection. That way, no one has to sort through those 150,000+ photos and videos to find the best of the best. I'll do that for them.

My college roommate Rachel Schroeder told me that is something her parents did that was a huge gift for her.

> My parents took all the slides they had and digitized them. They then put everything on a thumb drive for me and my sisters. There are about 1,200 photos included. It has pictures of my parents, siblings, grandparents, and great-grandparents.
>
> They did it about twenty years ago, not necessarily as preparation for death, but to make sure the photos were shared, kept, and accessible. They saw that people weren't going to pull out a slide carousel anymore, so they digitized everything. Now, all of it is on my dad's Mac. He also gave each of us kids a USB drive with all the photos labeled. If I'm looking for a photo of my father, I'll see "Phil, six years old," "Phil at school," and so on.
>
> They included their annual Christmas cards and newspaper articles, like when he was ordained in seminary. It's a valuable historical record for the family. It's really precious.

Rachel and her parents currently use these photos all of the time to make gifts or celebrate occasions. However, we can all imagine what a wonderful historical collection this will be to pass along to the next generations.

Questions to Ask Myself About My Financial Accounts

- Do I have a personal checking account?

- Do I have a personal savings account?

- Do I have any business banking accounts or merchant accounts? Have I created an end-of-life plan for my business affairs?

- Do I own a complex business which requires a whole set of instructions and its own estate planning?

- Do I have a 401(k) retirement account?

- Do I have an Individual Retirement Account (IRA)?

- Do I have a pension plan?

- What is the status of my Social Security benefits?

- Do I have a brokerage account for stocks or other investments?

- Do I have a 529 education savings plan?

- Do I have a Health Savings Account (HSA)?

- Do I have a Flexible Spending Account (FSA)?

- Do I have a credit card account?

- Do I have any personal loans?

- Do I have a home mortgage?

- Do I have a Home Equity Line of Credit (HELOC)?

- Do I have a life insurance policy?

- Do I have an annuity?

- Do I have a revocable or irrevocable trust?

- Do I have any debts or liabilities, such as student loans, auto loans, or personal loans?

- Do I have a safe deposit box?

Questions to Ask Myself About My Automatic Subscriptions and Memberships

- Do I have any automatic subscriptions for meal kits or groceries from companies such as HelloFresh or Blue Apron? Do I have subscriptions from local markets or grocery stores that deliver?

- Do I have any automatic subscriptions for streaming services from companies such as Netflix, Disney, Hulu, or Spotify?

- Do I have any automatic subscriptions for beauty or grooming products from companies such as Ipsy, Birchbox, or Dollar Shave Club?

- Do I have any automatic subscriptions for health or wellness products from companies such as Ritual or GNC Pro Access?

- Do I have any automatic subscriptions for clothing or accessories from companies such as Stitch Fix, Nuuly, or Menlo Club?

- Do I have any automatic subscriptions for books or magazines from companies such as Book of the Month?

- Do I have any automatic subscriptions for pet supplies from companies such as BarkBox or CatLadyBox?

- Do I have any automatic subscriptions for alcohol or beverages from companies such as Shaker & Spoon Cocktail Club or Trade Coffee?

- Do I have any automatic subscriptions for snacks or specialty foods from companies such as MunchPak, Universal Yums, or Fit Snack?

- Do I have any automatic subscriptions for fitness products from companies such as MuscleBox or FabFitFun?

- Do I have a gym membership that automatically renews?

Questions to Ask Myself About Household Details

- Do I have any utility services, such as electricity, gas, water, trash/recycling, or internet/phone services?

- Do I have any home maintenance services, such as security systems, HVAC maintenance, pest control, landscaping, or snow removal?

- Do I have any property and homeowner's insurance policies, such as homeowner's insurance or flood insurance?

- Do I have any financial and legal documents relating to tenancy of my rented home, such as lease or rental agreements, maintenance records, or security deposit receipts?

- Do I have any financial and legal documents relating to my home or other property I own, including mortgage information, property taxes, or homeowners association (HOA) details?

- Do I have any miscellaneous household information, such as mail forwarding, post office box information, home inventory, or service contracts?

Questions to Ask Myself About My Digital Life

- Do I have any digital financial accounts, such as PayPal, Venmo, or cryptocurrency wallets?

- Do I have any other financial management accounts that are not listed in the Financial Accounts section of this worksheet?

- Do I have any social media accounts, such as Facebook, Instagram, or LinkedIn?

- Do I have any email and communication accounts, such as Gmail, Outlook, Yahoo Mail, or WhatsApp?

- Do I have any entertainment and media accounts, such as Netflix, Hulu, Spotify, Kindle, or Audible?

- Do I have any shopping and subscriptions accounts, such as Amazon, eBay, Etsy, subscription boxes, or meal kit services?

- Do I have any personal and professional documentation stored in services like Google Drive, Dropbox, iCloud, or password managers?

- Do I have any health and wellness accounts, such as MyChart, Fitbit, Apple Health, or Zocdoc?

- Do I have any travel and transportation accounts, such as Expedia, Uber, Lyft, Airbnb, or airline/hotel loyalty programs?

- Do I have any home management accounts, such as Google Home, Amazon Alexa, Ring, smart thermostats, or utility accounts?

- Do I have any education and learning accounts, such as Coursera, Khan Academy, Blackboard, or school portals?

- Do I have any legal and identity management accounts, such as online storage for wills, contracts, deeds, or government portals?

- Do I have any business and professional services accounts, such as Upwork, Fiverr, Microsoft 365, or Adobe Creative Cloud?

- Do I have any photography and digital memories stored in services like Google Photos, Shutterfly, Flickr, or social media albums?

- Do I have any gaming and virtual world accounts, such as Steam, PlayStation Network, Xbox Live, or virtual goods, including NFTs?

- Do I have any memberships and rewards programs, such as airline loyalty programs, Costco, AAA road service, gym memberships, or club memberships?

- Do I have a collection of digital photos that I need to organize?

Note: There may be some overlap here since our digital lives are intertwined with the financial, subscription, and household parts of our lives. We just want to make sure all the bases are covered in a way that makes the most sense to you.

☑ Section 4 Worksheet: Checklist and Fill In

1. INSTRUCTIONS ON MY FINANCIAL ACCOUNTS

I have completed written instructions on all of my financial accounts:

❏ I have made a complete list with the type of account, financial institution, account numbers, passwords, and other essential information.

These documents can be found: _____

❏ **I have a checking account.**

The bank or other financial institution is: _____

Their website is: _____

My login name and password can be found here: _____

_____

❏ **I have a savings account.**

The bank or other financial institution is: _____

Their website is: _____

My login name and password can be found here: _____

_____

❏ **I have business financial accounts and merchant accounts.**

The designated executor for my business estate is: _____

Their contact information is: _____

_____

My legacy plan for my business can be found here: _____

_____

_____

❏ **I have a 401(k) retirement account.**

The financial institution is: _____

Their website is: _____

My login name and password can be found here: _____

_____

❏ **I have an Individual Retirement Account (IRA).**

The financial institution is: _____

Their website is: _____

My login name and password can be found here: _____

_____

❏ **I have a Pension Plan.**

The financial institution is: _____

Their website is: _____

My login name and password can be found here: _____

_____

❏ **I have Social Security Benefits.**

My SSN can be found here: _____

Other benefit information can be found here: _____

My login name and password can be found here: _____

_____

❏ **I have a brokerage account for stocks or other investments.**

The financial institution is: _____

Their website is: _____

My login name and password can be found here: _____

_____

❏ **I have a 529 education savings plan.**

The financial institution is: _____

Their website is: _____

My login name and password can be found here: _____

_____

❏ **I have a Health Savings Account (HSA).**

The financial institution is: _____

Their website is: _____

My login name and password can be found here: _____

_____

❏ **I have a Flexible Spending Account (FSA).**

The financial institution is: _____

Their website is: _____

My login name and password can be found here: _____

_____

❏ **I have a credit card account.**

The financial institution is: _____

Their website is: _____

My login name and password can be found here: _____

_____

❏ **I have another credit card account.**

The financial institution is: _____

Their website is: _____

My login name and password can be found here: _____

_____

❏ I have another credit card account.

The financial institution is: _____

Their website is: _____ _____

My login name and password can be found here: _____

_____

❏ I have a personal loan.

The financial institution is: _____

Their website is: _____

My login name and password can be found here: _____

_____

❏ I have a home mortgage.

The financial institution is: _____

Their website is: _____

My login name and password can be found here: _____

_____

❏ I have a Home Equity Line of Credit (HELOC).

The financial institution is: _____

Their website is: _____

My login name and password can be found here: _____

_____

❏ I have a life insurance policy.

The insurer is: _____

Their website is: _____

My login name and password can be found here: _____

_____

❏ **I have an annuity.**

The financial institution is: _____

Their website is: _____

My login name and password can be found here: _____

_____

❏ **I have a revocable or irrevocable trust.**

The financial institution is: _____

Their website is: _____

My login name and password can be found here: _____

_____

❏ **I have a** _____**financial account.**

The financial institution is: _____

Their website is: _____

My login name and password can be found here: _____

_____

❏ **I have a** _____**financial account.**

The financial institution is: _____

Their website is: _____

My login name and password can be found here: _____

_____

❏ **I have a** _____ **financial account.**

The financial institution is: _____

Their website is: _____

My login name and password can be found here: _____

_____

❏ I have debts or liabilities.

The type of debt is: _____

The financial institution is: _____

Their website is: _____

My login name and password can be found here: _____

_____

❏ I have other debts or liabilities.

The type of debt is: _____

The financial institution is: _____

Their website is: _____

My login name and password can be found here: _____

_____

❏ I have a safe deposit box.

The location is: _____

The following person has the key or access information: _____

_____

2. INSTRUCTIONS ON MY SUBSCRIPTIONS AND MEMBERSHIPS

I have completed written instructions for all of my automatic subscriptions and memberships:

❏ I have made a complete list with the type of account, account numbers, passwords, and other essential information so these accounts can be canceled.

These documents can be found _____

I haven't had a chance to formally document all of my subscription accounts, but here is a quick checklist that I hope will be helpful to you in the meantime:

Meal Kits and Groceries

❏ I have an automatic subscription for a meal kit.

The company is: _____

Their website is: _____

To cancel, my login name and password can be found here: _____

_____

Streaming Services

❏ I have an automatic subscription for a streaming service.

The company is: _____

Their website is: _____

To cancel, my login name and password can be found here: _____

_____

Beauty and Grooming

❏ I have an automatic subscription for beauty or grooming products.

The company is: _____

Their website is: _____

To cancel, my login name and password can be found here: _____

_____

Health and Wellness

❏ I have an automatic subscription for health or wellness products.

The company is: _____

Their website is: _____

To cancel, my login name and password can be found here: _____

_____

Clothing and Accessories

❏ I have an automatic subscription for clothing or accessories.

The company is: _____

Their website is: _____

To cancel, my login name and password can be found here: _____

_____

Books and Magazines

❏ I have an automatic subscription for books or magazines.

The company is: _____

Their website is: _____

To cancel, my login name and password can be found here: _____

_____

Pet Supplies

❏ I have an automatic subscription for pet supplies.

The company is: _____

Their website is: _____

To cancel, my login name and password can be found here: _____

_____

Alcohol and Beverages

❏ I have an automatic subscription for alcohol or beverages.

The company is: _____

Their website is: _____

To cancel, my login name and password can be found here: _____

_____

Snacks and Specialty Foods

❏ I have an automatic subscription for snacks or specialty foods.

The company is: _____

Their website is: _____

To cancel, my login name and password can be found here: _____

_____

Fitness

❏ I have an automatic subscription for fitness products.

The company is: _____

Their website is: _____

To cancel, my login name and password can be found here: _____

_____

Gym Membership

❏ I have a gym membership that is automatically renewed.

The company is: _____

Their website is: _____

To cancel, my login name and password can be found here: _____

_____

3. INSTRUCTIONS ON MY HOUSEHOLD DETAILS

I have completed written instructions:

❏ I have made my household plans.

These documents can be found _____

I haven't had a chance to formally document all of my wishes, but here is a quick checklist and some of my thoughts that I hope will be helpful to you in the meantime:

Household Financial and Legal Documents

❏ I have financial and legal documents, such as mortgage information, property taxes, or homeowners association (HOA) details, or lease or rental agreements.

The type of document is: _____

The financial institution or authority is: _____

Here is their website and contact information: _____

My account or document number is: _____

Details about how I make payments can be found here: _____

_____

The type of document is: _____

The financial institution or authority is: _____

Here is their website and contact information: _____

My account or document number is: _____

Details about how I make payments can be found here: _____

_____

Utility Services

❏ I have utility services, such as electricity, gas, water, trash/recycling, or internet/ phone services.

The type of service is: _____

The company is: _____

Here is their website and contact information: _____

_____

My account number is: _____

Details about how I make payments can be found here: _____

_____

The type of service is: _____

The company is: _____

Here is their website and contact information: _____

My account number is: _____

Details about how I make payments can be found here: _____

_____

The type of service is: _____

The company is: _____

Here is their website and contact information: _____

_____

My account number is: _____

Details about how I make payments can be found here: _____

_____

Home Maintenance Services

❏ **I have home maintenance services, such as security systems, HVAC maintenance, pest control, landscaping, or snow removal.**

The type of service is: _____

The company is: _____

Here is their website and contact information: _____

_____

My account number is: _____

Details about how I make payments can be found here: _____

_____

_____

Property and Homeowner's Insurance Policies

❏ **I have property and homeowner's insurance policies, such as homeowner's insurance or flood insurance.**

The type of policy is: _____

The insurance provider is: _____

Here is their website and contact information: _____

My policy number is: _____

Details about how I make payments can be found here: _____

_____

The type of policy is: _____

The insurance provider is: _____

Here is their website and contact information: _____

_____

My policy number is: _____

Details about how I make payments can be found here: _____

_____

Miscellaneous Household Information

❏ **I have miscellaneous household information to share, such as a post office box, home inventory, or service contracts.**

The type of service is: _____

The service provider or location is: _____

Here is their website and contact information: _____

_____

Access details or instructions can be found here: _____

The type of service is: _____

The service provider or location is: _____

Here is their website and contact information: _____

_____

Access details or instructions can be found here: _____

4. INSTRUCTIONS ON MY DIGITAL LIFE

I have completed written instructions:

❏ I have made my digital plans.

These documents can be found _____

> **I haven't had a chance to formally document all of my wishes, but here is a quick checklist and some of my thoughts that I hope will be helpful to you in the meantime:**

Financial Management Accounts

❏ **I have financial management accounts, such as online banking, investment accounts, budgeting tools, or cryptocurrency wallets.**

The account type is: _____

The company/platform is: _____

Here is their website and contact information: _____

_____

My login name and password can be found here: _____

❏ **I have financial management accounts, such as online banking, investment accounts, budgeting tools, or cryptocurrency wallets.**

The account type is: _____

The company/platform is: _____

Here is their website and contact information: _____

_____

My login name and password can be found here: _____

_____

Note that there may be some overlap here since our digital lives are intertwined with our financial, subscriptions, and household parts of our lives. I'm just making sure all the bases are covered in a way that might make sense to you as you are handling these digital assets.

❏ **I have financial management accounts, such as online banking, investment accounts, budgeting tools, or cryptocurrency wallets.**

The account type is: _____

The company/platform is: _____

Here is their website and contact information: _____

_____

My login name and password can be found here: _____

_____

Social Media Accounts

❏ **I have social media accounts, such as Facebook, Instagram, or LinkedIn.**

The account type is: _____

The company/platform is: _____

Here is their website and contact information: _____

My login name and password can be found here: _____

_____

❏ **I have social media accounts, such as Facebook, Instagram, or LinkedIn.**

The account type is: _____

The company/platform is: _____

Here is their website and contact information: _____

_____

My login name and password can be found here: _____

_____

❏ **I have social media accounts, such as Facebook, Instagram, or LinkedIn.**

The account type is: _____

The company/platform is: _____

Here is their website and contact information: _____

_____

My login name and password can be found here: _____

_____

Email and Communication Accounts

❏ **I have email and communication accounts, such as Gmail, Outlook, Yahoo Mail, or WhatsApp.**

The account type is: _____

The company/platform is: _____

Here is their website and contact information: _____

_____

My login name and password can be found here: _____

❏ **I have email and communication accounts, such as Gmail, Outlook, Yahoo Mail, or WhatsApp.**

The account type is: _____

The company/platform is: _____

Here is their website and contact information: _____

_____

My login name and password can be found here: _____

_____

❏ **I have email and communication accounts, such as Gmail, Outlook, Yahoo Mail, or WhatsApp.**

The account type is: _____

The company/platform is: _____

Here is their website and contact information: _____

_____

My login name and password can be found here: _____

_____

Entertainment and Media Accounts

❏ **I have entertainment and media accounts, such as Netflix, Hulu, Spotify, Kindle, or Audible.**

The account type is: _____

The company/platform is: _____

Here is their website and contact information: _____

_____

My login name and password can be found here: _____

_____

❑ **I have entertainment and media accounts, such as Netflix, Hulu, Spotify, Kindle, or Audible.**

The account type is: _____

The company/platform is: _____

Here is their website and contact information: _____

_____

My login name and password can be found here: _____

_____

❑ **I have entertainment and media accounts, such as Netflix, Hulu, Spotify, Kindle, or Audible.**

The account type is: _____

The company/platform is: _____

Here is their website and contact information: _____

_____

My login name and password can be found here: _____

_____

Shopping and Subscription Accounts

❑ **I have shopping and subscription accounts, such as Amazon, eBay, Etsy, subscription boxes, or meal kit services.**

The account type is: _____

The company/platform is: _____

Here is their website and contact information: _____

_____

My login name and password can be found here: _____

_____

❏ **I have shopping and subscription accounts, such as Amazon, eBay, Etsy, subscription boxes, or meal kit services.**

The account type is: _____

The company/platform is: _____

Here is their website and contact information: _____

_____

My login name and password can be found here: _____

_____

❏ **I have shopping and subscription accounts, such as Amazon, eBay, Etsy, subscription boxes, or meal kit services.**

The account type is: _____

The company/platform is: _____

Here is their website and contact information: _____

_____

My login name and password can be found here: _____

_____

Personal and Professional Documentation

❏ **I have personal and professional documentation stored in services like Google Drive, Dropbox, iCloud, or password managers.**

The account type is: _____

The company/platform is: _____

Here is their website and contact information: _____

_____

My login name and password can be found here: _____

_____

❑ **I have personal and professional documentation stored in services like Google Drive, Dropbox, iCloud, or password managers.**

The account type is: _____

The company/platform is: _____

Here is their website and contact information: _____

_____

My login name and password can be found here: _____

_____

❑ **I have personal and professional documentation stored in services like Google Drive, Dropbox, iCloud, or password managers.**

The account type is: _____

The company/platform is: _____

Here is their website and contact information: _____

_____

My login name and password can be found here: _____

_____

Health and Wellness Accounts

❑ **I have health and wellness accounts, such as MyChart, Fitbit, Apple Health, or Zocdoc.**

The account type is: _____

The company/platform is: _____

Here is their website and contact information: _____

_____

My login name and password can be found here: _____

_____

❏ **I have health and wellness accounts, such as MyChart, Fitbit, Apple Health, or Zocdoc.**

The account type is: _____

The company/platform is: _____

Here is their website and contact information: _____

_____

My login name and password can be found here: _____

_____

❏ **I have health and wellness accounts, such as MyChart, Fitbit, Apple Health, or Zocdoc.**

The account type is: _____

The company/platform is: _____

Here is their website and contact information: _____

_____

My login name and password can be found here: _____

_____

Travel and Transportation Accounts

❏ **I have travel and transportation accounts, such as Expedia, Uber, Lyft, Airbnb, or airline/hotel loyalty programs.**

The account type is: _____

The company/platform is: _____

Here is their website and contact information: _____

_____

My login name and password can be found here: _____

_____

❏ **I have travel and transportation accounts, such as Expedia, Uber, Lyft, Airbnb, or airline/hotel loyalty programs.**

The account type is: _____

The company/platform is: _____

Here is their website and contact information: _____

_____

My login name and password can be found here: _____

_____

❏ **I have travel and transportation accounts, such as Expedia, Uber, Lyft, Airbnb, or airline/hotel loyalty programs.**

The account type is: _____

The company/platform is: _____

Here is their website and contact information: _____

_____

My login name and password can be found here: _____

_____

Home Management Accounts

❏ **I have home management accounts, such as Google Home, Amazon Alexa, Ring, smart thermostats, or utility accounts.**

The account type is: _____

The company/platform is: _____

Here is their website and contact information: _____

_____

My login name and password can be found here: _____

_____

❏ **I have home management accounts, such as Google Home, Amazon Alexa, Ring, smart thermostats, or utility accounts.**

The account type is: _____

The company/platform is: _____

Here is their website and contact information: _____

_____

My login name and password can be found here: _____

_____

❏ **I have home management accounts, such as Google Home, Amazfzon Alexa, Ring, smart thermostats, or utility accounts.**

The account type is: _____

The company/platform is: _____

Here is their website and contact information: _____

_____

My login name and password can be found here: _____

_____

Education and Learning Accounts

❏ **I have education and learning accounts, such as Coursera, Khan fAcademy, Blackboard, or school portals.**

The account type is: _____

The company/platform is: _____

Here is their website and contact information: _____

_____

My login name and password can be found here: _____

_____

❑ **I have education and learning accounts, such as Coursera, Khan Academy, Blackboard, or school portals.**

The account type is: _____

The company/platform is: _____

Here is their website and contact information: _____

_____

My login name and password can be found here: _____

_____

❑ **I have education and learning accounts, such as Coursera, Khan Academy, Blackboard, or school portals.**

The account type is: _____

The company/platform is: _____

Here is their website and contact information: _____

_____

My login name and password can be found here: _____

_____

Legal and Identity Management Accounts

❑ **I have legal and identity management accounts, such as fonline storage for wills, contracts, deeds, or government portals.**

The account type is: _____

The company/platform is: _____

Here is their website and contact information: _____

_____

My login name and password can be found here: _____

_____

❑ **I have legal and identity management accounts, such as online storage for wills, contracts, deeds, or government portals.**

The account type is: _____

The company/platform is: _____

Here is their website and contact information: _____

_____

My login name and password can be found here: _____

_____

❑ **I have legal and identity management accounts, such as online storage for wills, contracts, deeds, or government portals.**

The account type is: _____

The company/platform is: _____

Here is their website and contact information: _____

_____

My login name and password can be found here: _____

_____

Business and Professional Services Accounts

❑ **I have business and professional services accounts, such as Upwork, Fiverr, Microsoft 365, or Adobe Creative Cloud.**

The account type is: _____

The company/platform is: _____

Here is their website and contact information: _____

_____

My login name and password can be found here: _____

_____

❏ **I have business and professional services accounts, such as Upwork, Fiverr, Microsoft 365, or Adobe Creative Cloud.**

The account type is: _____

The company/platform is: _____

Here is their website and contact information: _____

_____

My login name and password can be found here: _____

_____

❏ **I have business and professional services accounts, such as Upwork, Fiverr, Microsoft 365, or Adobe Creative Cloud.**

The account type is: _____

The company/platform is: _____

Here is their website and contact information: _____

_____

My login name and password can be found here: _____

_____

Photography and Digital Memories

❏ **I have photography and digital memories stored in services like Google Photos, Shutterfly, or Flickr, or in social media albums.**

The account type is: _____

The company/platform is: _____

Here is their website and contact information: _____

_____

My login name and password can be found here: _____

_____

❏ **I have photography and digital memories stored in services like Google Photos, Shutterfly, or Flickr, or in social media albums.**

The account type is: _____

The company/platform is: _____

Here is their website and contact information: _____

_____

My login name and password can be found here: _____

_____

❏ **I have photography and digital memories stored in services like Google Photos, Shutterfly, or Flickr, or in social media albums.**

The account type is: _____

The company/platform is: _____

Here is their website and contact information: _____

_____

My login name and password can be found here: _____

_____

❏ **I have photography and digital memories stored on my desktop computer.**

These can be found here: _____

Gaming and Virtual World Accounts

❏ **I have gaming and virtual world accounts, such as Steam, PlayStation Network, Xbox Live, or virtual goods, including NFTs.**

The account type is: _____

The company/platform is: _____

Here is their website and contact information: _____

_____

My login name and password can be found here: _____

_____

❑ **I have gaming and virtual world accounts, such as Steam, PlayStation Network, Xbox Live, or virtual goods, including NFTs.**

The account type is: _____

The company/platform is: _____

Here is their website and contact information: _____

_____

My login name and password can be found here: _____

_____

❑ **I have gaming and virtual world accounts, such as Steam, PlayStation Network, Xbox Live, or virtual goods, including NFTs.**

The account type is: _____

The company/platform is: _____

Here is their website and contact information: _____

My login name and password can be found here: _____

_____

Memberships and Rewards Programs

❑ **I have memberships and rewards programs, such as airline loyalty programs, Costco, AAA road service, gym memberships, or club memberships.**

The account type is: _____

The company/platform is: _____

Here is their website and contact information: _____

_____

My login name and password can be found here: _____

_____

❏ **I have memberships and rewards programs, such as airline loyalty programs, Costco, AAA road service, gym memberships, or club memberships.**

The account type is: _____

The company/platform is: _____

Here is their website and contact information: _____

_____

My login name and password can be found here: _____

_____

❏ **I have memberships and rewards programs, such as airline loyalty programs, Costco, AAA road service, gym memberships, or club memberships.**

The account type is: _____

The company/platform is: _____

Here is their website and contact information: _____

_____

My login name and password can be found here: _____

_____

The Art of Decluttering and Memory Keeping Before You're Gone

"The things you own end up owning your loved ones when you're gone. Lighten their load by lightening your own."

—Anonymous

I'm on This Journey, Too!

As I've been working on this book and on my own end-of-life planning, one of the biggest areas of personal focus for me has been the process of clearing and sorting *stuff*.

I've always been the archivist in the family. I'm the one who cataloged all the historical family photos and who bought the fire safe to store birth certificates, savings bonds, and other legal papers. I've got boxes of my son's creative writing poems, letters from my mom, and every homemade greeting card ever made for me. I have dozens of three-ring binders, ordered chronologically, filled with memorabilia and family history. I have wedding videos, birthday videos, and every video from every school play my son was ever in.

I have my grandmother's jewelry, boxes of my son's childhood books, glassware and collectibles from my grandmother's china closet, more than a hundred vintage hats, and so much more.

I'm going to stop there because it is pretty darn stressful just to write about this! You see, in my quest to save the important stuff, I saved *everything*.

And if I were to die today, no one would be able to find anything of importance because there is so much of everything.

Imagine going to a huge junkyard where there are acres and acres of discarded items, and you know that there are real treasures somewhere in there—maybe even gold trinkets!— but you know it would be nearly impossible to find them.

That's my world right now. It is easy to feel shame and stress. It is easy to feel overwhelmed, too.

Thankfully, I know there is a way to approach the sifting and sorting with mindfulness and appreciation, rather than with blame and guilt.

Echoing in my mind is a beautiful conversation I had recently with end-of-life doula Kat Primeau, who talked about going through our belongings as a gentle, contemplative practice in which we can bring joy and mindfulness to the stuff we are keeping, even as we are letting some of it go.

She says, "Decluttering is a transformational experience in which you get to be present with your belongings, review and celebrate your life, and consciously leave a lighter footprint."

I also love that Kat reminded me that I could see the sorting process as an important duty, not a punishment for having all this stuff. She said, "These things come into our lives, and we can stash them away or trash them—or we can smartly and conscientiously attend to them. We can be present with them and consider how we want to leave things for future generations."

When I spoke with Kat, she truly emphasized the joy that could be present in the process.

It reminded me of something my son said to me a few years ago when I was having a hard time clearing out some stuff. He said, "Mom, think about it this way. If you weren't getting rid of stuff, everything would probably stay stashed away in drawers and closets forever. You might never even look at it again. This way, you are holding every item at least once more. You're remembering the story of it. You're connecting to why it was meaningful to you."

He added, "Deciding to part ways with something may be painful, but the act of remembering the story behind it or holding it up under the light is a way to cherish something you've been neglecting. Getting rid of things can allow you to really enjoy them."

My son is one big reason I want to go through this process. There's no way I want to leave him with all these things. I wouldn't want him to have to waste any amount of his life on my life's possessions.

Kat is right: We accumulated this stuff; it is our duty to figure out what to do with it. And hopefully, as we do that, we can be grateful for every item we touch. The process can be a beautiful walk down memory lane. We just don't have to pick up every item and carry it with us the rest of the way!

This process can be broken down into two steps: Memory Keeping and Death Cleaning. Start in either place—or mix and match in a way that works best for you.

Memory Keeping

What Is This?

As we think about the last sections of our lives and what we want to leave behind, one of the first things that often comes to mind is the question, "What tangible items do I want to leave behind and make sure are preserved?"

I don't claim to be any kind of professional organizer or death cleaner. (You probably gathered that from my previous story!)

However, I'm on this journey with you, and I too am exploring the path of sifting through belongings to organize them for my loved ones. Remember what I said about how it feels like right now there is a huge junkyard where no one would ever find the treasures? My goal is to make it obvious, streamlined, and simple for others—like leaving a treasure chest filled with the goodies so they know everything else is optional.

As the saying goes, "One man's trash is another's treasure." So, it is up to you (and your loved ones) to discern what matters and what is worth preserving for the future.

Below are some areas to consider when determining what might (or might not) be important for your loved ones.

As you are sorting through things, remember to have conversations with the people in your life to see if your best guesses about who-would-care-about-what are right.

As well, remember that young people in your life may not yet have a sense of what could be important to them down the road. Sometimes people become more interested in the past as they reach middle age. So, if your fifteen-year-old niece tells you she isn't sentimental and doesn't want anything old, consider setting aside a small piece of jewelry or a small family heirloom just in case.

What to Keep and What to Toss: Some Categories to Consider

Take a look at the list of categories of personal items and artifacts below. For each, you may want to consider what you own that fits into that category. You could even make a written list of the most valuable or standout items in each category. Then, further consider whether anyone in your life might want any of these items as a keepsake after you pass. You may not know the answer to this question right off, and that's okay. Just ask! Yep, that's right.

You can show your list to your sister, your cousin, or your BFF, and ask, "Would you want any of these things once I pass away?"

- Personal Items
- Jewelry
- Clothing
- Accessories
- Documents and Papers
- Letters and Cards
- Diaries and Journals
- Certificates and Awards
- Legal Documents
- Photographs and Media
- Home Videos
- Audio Recordings
- Hobbies and Collections
- Books
- Music
- Art Supplies
- Crafts
- Furniture and Decor

- Textiles
- Artwork, including paintings, sculpture, and other creative media
- Family Heirlooms
- Historical Artifacts
- Keepsakes from Special Events
- Wedding Keepsakes
- Birth and Baby Keepsakes
- Travel Souvenirs
- Digital Keepsakes
- Emails and Messages
- Social Media Content
- Digital Archives
- Financial Keepsakes
- Coins and Currency
- Stocks and Bonds
- Memorabilia, including sports and entertainment

❤🔍 USEFUL TOOLS:

Create a Legacy Drive

Think about creating a "Legacy Drive," an external hard drive or thumb drive filled with a digitized collection of curated photos including the "Best Of" from your life along with other historical photos you have. Perhaps choose the best hundred from your life. Add in ten or fifteen great videos or home movies. Also digitize any important family papers, certificates, or legal documents, including your will and other notarized documents. Create easy-to-access folders and save all of this on an external hard drive that is the size of a small paperback. Aside from valuable heirlooms and artworks, this could be the most important item you pass down!

Consider acquiring an extra external hard drive or two to use as backup storage, as well as perhaps a cloud storage location for your data; extra hard drives can be stored in a location away from your residence in case of fire or flood, such as in a safe deposit box or at your workplace. The price of external hard drives has notably declined in recent years, and it's worth taking extra care in the safekeeping of historical records and memories that are irreplaceable.

Decluttering to Lighten Your Life—and Make It Easy on Your Loved Ones

Letting Go of Stuff Now Can Be a Relief

Most of us have had the experience of getting rid of unused or unwanted belongings and having a sense of expansiveness and joy afterward. There's something about decluttering that releases energy!

Decluttering and organizing your belongings can obviously simplify your life, and it greatly reduces the burden on your loved ones after you are gone. Most professional organizers will encourage you to spend time sorting through things so that you keep only those that truly matter to you, have practical use, or are valuable. One of the most well-known declutterers is Marie Kondo, who has a rather famous rule for sorting our things: "Ask yourself if it sparks joy."

Here Are Some Other Important Things to Keep in Mind:

- Begin this process as soon as possible. Clearing out our homes can be a gift to ourselves that we enjoy the rest of our lives.

- Choose a time when you feel energized and positive to sort through your things. It can be a challenging task, so you want to feel at your best when starting out.

- Keep things that you use frequently and that are practical in your life.

- Keep things that are meaningful to you emotionally or that may have significance to someone you love.

- If you are keeping special things to pass on to others, consider sharing this information with them and telling them the stories that go along with the items. (Be sure your wishes about what happens with those things are clearly documented!)

- As you are sorting through your things, take the time to clearly mark boxes that contain essential items versus the things you love but no one else will.

- Mark boxes for all the things you want to donate or give away, perhaps labeling each by category.

- Consider my idea of a Legacy Drive: a digital collection of curated photos, memorabilia, and documents. This is a great way to make them available to others, but in a way that doesn't take up a lot of space. See the tip on page 138!

- If there are items around your house that you are still using and want to keep as long as you can, but you know you want that item to go to someone special, think about marking items with labels underneath. Just keep an eye out if you tell people you are doing this: I've had some people tell me that others switched the labels!

- Consider hosting a party where people have the opportunity to choose sentimental items from things you own. This way you get to experience their joy now. See the expert tip on page 142.

- Check out the Resource Directory for this section for some helpful books and websites on decluttering.

·☼· EXPERT TIP:

Get the Clan Together for Annual Family Spring Cleaning

"Last year, my brother and I knew it was time to move my dad out of his house in Chicago and closer to my brother and me and on the West Coast so we could help him out more. Arriving to help him pack, I was blindsided by the mess and emotional weight of sorting through decades of memories: boxes of memorabilia, paperwork, and toys, as well as an entire garage filled with tools. Alone and on a tight timeline, the process was overwhelming and heartbreaking. I encourage everyone to commit to annual spring cleaning, enlisting the help of our families, to gradually manage the emotional and physical burden of possessions, thereby preventing such trauma."

—Shawn Buttner, high performance coach and podcaster

For Family Archivists

If you are the keeper of family history and you are overwhelmed by boxes of important papers, journals, photographs, and other family memorabilia, enlist the help of the family member most likely to become your successor from the next generation and have that future family archivist help you sort through things.

For Writers, Musicians, Artists

You may need to hire an attorney who specializes in intellectual property (IP) estate planning, which includes copyrighted materials for writers, musicians, and other creators.

They will make sure that your creative works are properly managed, protected, and distributed according to your wishes.

If that is too much for the level of your artistic endeavors, consider requesting that someone in your family—hopefully someone in the next generation—handle this.

If you are not interested in your artistic work living on past your own lifetime, please make sure you clearly state your wishes for its distribution to loved ones to do with what they wish or for its disposal.

If you are leaving specific family and friends your artwork in your will, it is a kindness to ask them in advance if they would like to have these pieces. Otherwise, they may feel burdened with an obligation to keep your artwork, even if it may not be to their taste.

For Collectors of Art, Coins, Antiques, Wine, or Other Valuables

If you are keeping your expensive or extensive collection until the day you die or have to move, please leave a list with a few places your loved ones can easily call to sell or donate it. If you are bequeathing a collection to someone, please make sure you leave plenty of documentation—including certificates of authentication and some expert contact information.

Host a Life Celebration and Give Away Treasured Belongings

Remember in Section Two, when I shared with you the idea of hosting a life celebration while you are still alive in lieu of a funeral? You can use that time with people you love to let them choose items of yours that they would like to have. It could actually be a beautiful ritual, with people you cherish selecting keepsakes one by one as they are visiting with you. It may be a chance to give them an object, tell them its story, and see the joy on the recipient's face as you pass along something you love.

Consider This: Meaningful Special Collections Deserve Extra Thought Right Now

My friend Alison Luterman is an amazing poet, essayist, and playwright who has been published and has performed in many places. When I told her I was working on this book, she immediately lit up with excitement for the importance of this kind of planning and preparation.

Alison shared two examples of deeply meaningful collections that she needs to make some plans for in case something happens to her or her husband. She said, "My husband, Lee, is a musician, and we have five keyboards, a full drum set, and tons of other musical instruments. These unique pieces are beautiful and were handmade with so much heart and skill. I love them. We have a big house, but he's older than me, and I could see outliving him and needing to downsize down the road. What am I going to do with these large, beautiful objects that are so personal and meaningful to him?"

She also shared with me that she is concerned about important collections of her own work. "Our creative work is like our babies; we want someone to care about them almost as much as we do, even when we're gone," Alison said. She continued:

> I have a manuscript of poems ready for publication, and I want it to be published whether I am here or not. If I got hit by a bus today, what would happen to that manuscript? Does my husband know where it is on my computer? Would he know how to get it published? He probably shouldn't handle it anyway, because he's not in the literary world.

And, oh—my laptop's organization is Byzantine! I know where things are and have my own system, but it's not clear to others. I should create instructions on accessing my laptop, locating the files, knowing which ones to publish, and suggesting where to send them.

That sounds like a great first step, right? But as Alison and I talked further, it became clear that even more thought would need to go into something like this for writers or artists of all kinds. She added this:

I don't have a literary executor or anyone designated for archiving my work or getting new work published. I could ask some of my poet friends, but they are all busy with their own work. I don't have any children, and I can't imagine that my nieces and nephews want the job of schlepping all my literary output along with them while they're building their own lives.

These decisions are delicate and difficult, without clear right answers. Knowing that my manuscript will not be lost would give me peace of mind. I've poured so much of my life energy and heart into it, and I want it to live on in the world.

Who knows? Maybe some descendant not yet born will have a keen interest in literary history or poetry. Perhaps a hundred years from now, they'll want to see what their ancestor was doing. I would hate for it all to get lost.

Consider This: It May Not Be Worth Saving

Many of us have spent a lifetime collecting furniture, art, and other stuff that feels really valuable to us. It might be true that these things are actually valuable. It is also possible that it may only be valuable to *us* because these are our treasures.

An acquaintance, Sue, told me a hard story. "When my mother-in-law died, we inherited her house filled with antiques and collectibles. For many years, she had been exclaiming about how incredibly valuable those items were. After she died, we had an appraiser come to the house, and it turned out that most of it wasn't worth anything. We were able to sell some of it, but in fact, we had to spend thousands of dollars to get it carted away—and that was after several weeks of my husband and his brother working full-time to clear out a lifetime's accumulation of mostly worthless junk. It was terribly draining and hard on everyone."

This is a good example of why we want to have things appraised so we know whether it is valuable only to us.

Celebrate All of Your Hard Work

You've done a lot of hard work and made some difficult choices about what to keep and what to let go of. Congratulations on reaching this phase of the planning. Now, it is time to reward yourself for all of your efforts.

Here are a few ways you can celebrate your clutter-free home:

- Enjoy the peaceful solitude by lighting some candles or playing music you love and relaxing in the beautiful space you've created. Maybe buy yourself that new work of fiction you've been wanting to read and get cozy in your clean space.

- Invite a couple of friends or family members over for some take-out dinner so they can admire all you've done to create a less cluttered space. Consider offering and giving away any last items that you think they might like!

- Buy some new towels, curtains, or a warm blanket to treat yourself to some luxury—but make sure you get rid of the old ones by donating them to your favorite animal shelter or charity!

Questions to Ask Myself About Sentimental or Family Keepsakes

- Have I done proper cleaning and clutter clearing so I can assess my belongings and earmark what should be saved and what can be donated upon my death?

- Have I decided whether I want to hire a clutter organizer to assist with this clearing or whether I will tackle it on my own?

- Have I had conversations with my family and friends about what items they would like to have when I pass?

- Are those preferences and requests noted in my official will?

- Is there someone in the next generation who loves family history and who might be willing to be the keeper of photos, documents, letters, and other historical papers?

- If some things are sentimental to me but not to others I know, can I find good homes for these things outside of my friends or family?

Questions to Ask Myself About Valuable Collections

- What collections do I own that have not been accounted for already in my will?

- Is this collection something that only has sentimental value to me, or is it objectively valuable?

- If it is sentimental, is there someone I know who would want this and who should be asked if they would like to receive it when I can no longer be its keeper?

- If none of my family or friends is interested in this collection, is there an organization or fellow collector(s) I can ask if they would want this?

- What is the value of this collection? Have I had the collection appraised? When was it last appraised?

- Do I have detailed records of the collection, including a list of items and their value?

- If this collection is valuable, have I designated in my will or trust who will receive the collection when I die?

- Have I noted for the beneficiaries any contact information for appraisers, curators, and specialized attorneys who may be of assistance in dealing with my collection?

- Have I had conversations with my heirs so they understand the value and significance of my collection and how to manage it?

☑ Section 5 Worksheet: Checklist and Fill In

☐ **I have created a prioritized list of types of collections or memories I want to organize: photos, keepsakes, artwork, jewelry, and so on.**

These documents can be found _____

_____

☐ **Before keeping, donating, or tossing anything meaningful or valuable, I've asked my loved ones if they would like these items bequeathed to them.**

Have these been noted elsewhere? Where? _____

_____

☐ **My valuable collections have been appraised and documented.**

These documents can be found _____

_____

☐ **My intellectual property collections (i.e., my original music, writing, art) have been evaluated, and I've noted which are financially valuable, sentimentally valuable, or only valuable to me.**

These documents can be found _____

_____

☐ **I've updated my will to include all of this information.**

These documents can be found _____

_____

Life Lessons and Wisdom I'd Like to Pass On to My Loved Ones

"The song is ended, but the melody lingers on."
—Irving Berlin

You Have Already Left a Beautiful Footprint on This Planet

You've Come So Far!

Remember at the beginning of this book when I encouraged you to consider the philosophy, "Leave not a trace?" If you've been tackling these end-of-life planning activities in the order I've presented them, you have made huge inroads to doing this. And I congratulate you. You've taken care of many of the essential areas that could have caused unintended anxiety, grief, and stress for your loved ones. You've stepped into a new place in your life. Do you feel it?

I hope you will pause as you are reading this and allow yourself to feel grateful that you are the type of person willing to do whatever it takes in order to leave this last gift behind. So many people know that they should take the responsible steps to plan for their end of life. But they don't do it.

As you are appreciating yourself, consider this: "What enables me to keep walking through this process, even though it is hard? How am I able to find self-discipline within myself? What motivates me?"

These are great questions to ponder because they will tell you a lot about your willingness and commitment to achieving big things in life.

Leaving a loving legacy is a huge thing to be proud about!

Sharing Your Life Story

Your Stories Matter—to You and to the People You Love

Those questions I asked you to ponder on the previous page are a hint of what is coming next!

We are going to turn our attention away from all of the gathering, clearing, sorting, and notarizing! We are going to look inside ourselves. This next step of the process is you are going to write or record some reflections on who you are, what you've learned, and what has been most important to you on the journey of your life.

Please don't skip this step!

In researching this book, one of the things that countless people expressed to me is their huge regret that they didn't have more stories or lessons written down about the person they loved who passed away. Time and again, people told me they wished they had interviewed their loved one or that that person had recorded stories and wisdom to be passed down to the next generations.

One of my colleagues at work, Babe Hoffarber Garcia, told me that her dad died when she was young. He was an only child and didn't have much family, so there weren't a lot of people who knew him. She said she has so many questions that she wishes she could ask him.

> I wonder about him all the time. I wish I could ask how he met my mother, what he thought of her, why he decided to get married, what it was like becoming a father, his political views. I'd love to know his interests—his favorite foods, music, movies. I'd like to know his happiest moments, his accomplishments, or if he had any regrets. I want to know his philosophy and outlook on life.
>
> I try to piece it together from things my mom tells me or from old yearbooks, but there's not a lot there. I really wish he had written these things down.

What Babe is saying is true for her, having lost her dad at such a young age. However, it is also true for many people whose parents or other loved ones die late in life, in their eighties or nineties. We may never think to ask our parents any of these kinds of questions, but after they die, we always long to know so much more.

Sometimes, even if we've heard bits and pieces of their stories throughout their lives, we may regret never having written down or recorded those stories. That is why it is such a huge gift to leave your stories behind!

🔍 USEFUL TOOLS:

Helpful Prompts to Share Your Wisdom

Facing a blank page (or computer screen) can be daunting when we want to leave behind some of our life lessons and stories. Having thoughtful writing prompts can make the process easy and enjoyable. That's why I've included a QR code below that links to dozens of questions you can choose from to begin to craft your ideas.

When his beloved dad was dying, Brendon Burchard interviewed him at his bedside. He's made all of those questions available for others to use.

> "Using the questions I've developed for interviewing loved ones can also serve as a powerful tool for your own self-reflection and legacy-building. By interviewing yourself, you can capture your thoughts, values, and experiences, creating a meaningful record for your children or spouse.
>
> This not only preserves your legacy but also provides your loved ones with deep insights into your life and beliefs, offering comfort and guidance in the future. It's a beautiful way to share your journey and lessons learned, ensuring your wisdom and love are passed down through generations."
>
> —Brendon Burchard, *New York Times* bestselling author
> and world-renowned high performance coach

Interview questions from high performance coach Brendon Burchard

Consider This: Get Support for Telling Your Story

You may feel like you're too young to write about these things now. Or you may hold the belief that no one in your life will care about your life stories. You may feel like it's too much to think about, or maybe you are hesitant because painful memories might arise. Please don't let any of these things stop you!

Consider what Babe Garcia said about her father dying. He was young and may not have considered that he would pass away and leave his daughter with so many unanswered questions.

I feel the same way about my grandfather. Even though he was in his eighties when he died, I was only in my twenties. I hadn't yet realized how incredibly important to me learning my grandpa's stories would become. Unfortunately, it wasn't until years later that I realized how little we knew about him.

He'd immigrated to the United States when he was sixteen, taking a ship all the way from a small town in Albania. He opened a coffee shop, married, had children—a whole life filled with hopes and dreams and accomplishments that were never documented. What a shame.

I'm glad that you are still reading this, and hopefully you are willing to capture your wisdom and stories for people who love you currently, as well as for those descendants who may not even be born yet!

Obviously, you can put pen to paper (or fingers to keyboard!) and capture your life's highlights all on your own. However, it can be difficult to face an entirely blank page! The worksheet at the end of this section will give you a good place to begin. I've compiled a short list of questions for you that will go a long way toward helping the people who love you feel even more connected to you and your story.

You may find that as you start to recall your favorite memories and proudest moments, you'll want to write even more. If so, I encourage you to take a look at the Useful Tool on the previous page to learn about using a set of interview questions developed by high performance coach Brendon Burchard. The QR code on that page links to that entire set of questions.

You can also shop for journals created especially for capturing legacy stories. Some of them are simply blank books, but others offer prompts. If you do use Brendon's prompts, perhaps you'll want to purchase a beautiful hardcover journal to write your responses in. Or you can simply type them out, print them, and file them in your Legacy Files.

If you love this kind of stuff and you want to go even further, there are a lot of companies that can help you compile your stories. They range in the level of personal support they offer—everything from weekly emailed questions that get compiled at the end to assigning you your own writer and designer who help you create a memoir.

Artist Gail Trunick, founder of Trunick Gallery, used a company called StoryWorth, and she loved the process. I've been a fan of Gail's work for several decades and have also loosely followed her story. She's got a magical backyard gallery in Burghill, Ohio, that includes a real train caboose to showcase her artwork, a theater (filled with sculpture audience members!) where she hosts artsy film nights, whimsical sculptures in almost every tree or bush, and a creative and colorful home filled with joy, color, and creations.

When Gail posted on social media that she was writing her life story with the help of weekly questions from a company called StoryWorth, I couldn't wait to get on the phone with her and hear more.

The first thing she said to me was, "Writing about my life has been like therapy. Such a rich process!" She added, "I was afraid I wouldn't be disciplined enough to sit down and do it every week because life gets so busy. Then, I got to where I did it at the same time on Sunday evenings, and I really looked forward to it. I would sit out on the porch with my feet up and simply type it up."

Gail told me that reflecting and writing about her life helped her to see it all in new ways. "I get to see that things that I hadn't thought were that interesting actually were! I've had a lot of those 'Wow, that is worth remembering' moments." (Those moments include surviving two tornados, and the time her mom cooked the Thanksgiving turkey in the pottery kiln!)

Gail explained, "Often, at first glance, the questions they ask seem mundane, but they turn into something much deeper when you're sharing them. My favorite Christmas memory might seem boring at first, but then as I write and remember, I realize how wonderful those experiences were. And if I were to die tomorrow, that would never be known."

StoryWorth invites you to tweak their questions or add your own so your stories can be specific to your life and what you want others to know. Gail is including stories and photos about her children's dad and their grandparents. She's going to put her mother's eulogy in there. It is such a great medium to use to organize family history you want to pass down.

It is also a way to convey our love to our children and grandchildren. Gail told me how she weaves this into her writings: "I added stories for my children about 'What makes me most proud of you.' And these are not things my children would probably guess! It's not about the books they've written, their travels, or other accomplishments. It is things like the time my son befriended another child who was being bullied, or how my daughter used her own money to anonymously buy and send flowers for anyone who was left out on Flower Day at school."

Perhaps most important of all, writing her stories has helped Gail to pause and reflect on the beauty and wonder of her life. She shared, "This process makes me look back and say, 'Hey, look at the richness that you've had. Look at all the experiences of your life.'"

She added, "It can be easy for all of us to focus on the hard stuff in our lives, but for most of us, there have been far more wonderful things. This story-writing process has gotten me to remember so many magnificent moments. It makes you look and say, 'I've lived a full and good life. When my time comes, I'm ready.'"

You can read more about Gail's process, how writing her stories has impacted her life, and how she hopes it will impact her children and grandchildren by clicking on the QR code below. You will be so surprised at some of the other things Gail learned from telling her story! On that page, I also share other great resources and tips for telling *your* story.

I was so energized after talking to Gail because *she* was lit up by the memories, stories, and insights pouring out of her! There are many surprising benefits to writing down our memories; I hope you will click over and get inspired.

Why reflecting on and writing about your life can be a huge gift to yourself and those who love *you*

Relishing Your Memories and Experiences Is a Gift

Consider This: Reflecting on Your Life Gives It Added Meaning

Philip Schroeder, the father of one of my childhood friends, Rachel, was a pastor in the Lutheran Church for many decades. I recently got to visit with him in Manhattan at Rachel's sixtieth birthday gathering. Philip and his wife Sharon were excited when I told them about this book project. They are both advocates of doing this kind of planning.

Philip said, "When I lead a funeral or memorial service, I like to include the person's life story in the service folder. It might be a few paragraphs or several pages, but it gives everyone a fuller idea of who the person was. I always encourage people to write that story themselves. The first draft is the hardest, but then you revisit it and add more, and over time, it grows. Even if it's never used for a service, it's a useful exercise and a valuable way for an older person to reflect on their life."

He paused and added this: "When you say, 'What a gift my life has been,' it's important to know what *made it* a gift. Reflecting on your marriage, children, and work, and how you've faced challenges throughout your life, brings that gift alive. It helps you understand and appreciate the profound gift that each of our lives truly is."

I think he is absolutely right. Just as Gail Trunick shared with us, sometimes our lives are moving so quickly that we simply are not pausing to reflect, and we may miss the deep meaning of our lessons and stories. We may even miss the gift it all has been.

I don't want that for you—or for your descendants. I want all of you to relish the gift of your life, your stories, and your wisdom. I want generations to come to be able to read your story and smile as they experience a sense of who you are and what matters to you.

Other Creative Ways to Share Your Lessons and Stories

Record Your Stories on Audio

If writing doesn't appeal to you, I want to encourage you to explore some other ways of sharing your wisdom, life lessons, and stories.

Sometimes it is easier to simply talk about our memories and what we've learned, especially if there is someone with us to ask us questions. StoryCorps is a wonderful company dedicated to helping people share their stories.

Before the pandemic, StoryCorps had recording booths set up in various places around the country. San Francisco's Main Library hosted a recording booth, and I had the chance to make special recordings with some of the most important people in my life! One of my favorite StoryCorps recordings is one I orchestrated between my then-ten-year-old son, his father, and his grandpa. It makes me tear up just thinking about how much that recording means to our family, because my young son got to pose questions to his Grandpa Bebop, who passed away a few years later.

StoryCorps no longer has these wonderful recording booths; however, their website is chock-full of resources and easy methods of doing these audio interviews with people you love. Ask one of your family members to try it out and interview you!

Sing or Act Out Your Life

My beau, Ian, has a talented musician mom. When she was in her seventies, she very intentionally pulled together some of the songs she'd written and put together a special CD of music she wrote and performed. While not quite an outright "memoir," these songs and her sweet voice share so much about her! They are musical memories of what touched her in her life.

My author friend, Allen, whom you met in a previous section when he talked about his over one hundred bow ties, celebrated his eightieth birthday with a musical show performed at a local theater. Allen gave us the story of his life as told through musicals he loves! It was one of the most amazing and personal celebrations I've ever experienced. I learned so much about Allen and was delighted at the creativity of his musical expression of his life story. Imagine that for years to come, his family will get to share those video recordings!

When I was having lunch recently at my favorite curry place with my friend Shawn Buttner, he reminded me of David Bowie's last creative work, the album *Blackstar*, which was a culmination of everything Bowie had learned as a musician and person.

Blackstar, which was released just a few days before Bowie's death, explored themes of mortality, spirituality, and transformation. Apparently, Bowie was aware of his terminal illness and used this creative project to reflect on his artistic legacy and his impending death.

If you are a musician or actor, would you want to create a beautiful opus of your own that showcases your philosophy on life or lessons learned along the way?

Maybe you're not a musician or actor, but perhaps these examples might inspire you to think of a creative way to tell your life story—perhaps using paintings, illustrations, collage, a handmade card deck of lessons learned, or another creative outlet.

Here Are Some Other Creative Ways to Tell Your Story and Share Wisdom

- **Visual Arts (Painting, Sculpture, Photography):** Create a retrospective exhibition (even if it is shown in your own house!) or compile a self-published book of art photos.

- **Literature (Writers, Poets, Playwrights):** Write a poetry or essay collection, or compile letters you've written and received.

- **Film and Theater:** Create a short play or documentary.

- **Dance and Performance Art:** Choreograph a dance or performance art project and have someone record it for you.

- **Multimedia and Technology:** Create a digital project that tells aspects of your life story or creatively documents part of your life.

Use your imagination to create something that feels just like *you*. Let this project be a joyful process of feeling the beauty of who you are and all the gifts you have been given. Not only will it delight the people you leave behind, it will fuel you to live more joyfully right now.

☀️ EXPERT TIP:

Document the Stories Behind Interesting Objects

I bet there are so many fascinating objects or pieces of art in your home that have meaningful stories behind them that only you know. Think about what a gift it would be to share those stories as part of the way you tell others about your life.

My friend and fellow coach Shawn Buttner once mused, "What has happened to the ancient art of storytelling? For instance, my wife's dad has a letter signed by Albert Einstein that he has framed on the wall. He wrote Einstein when he was a kid and got a letter back! What's the story behind that? We want to keep that letter and pass it on to future generations. But wouldn't it be so great to know the story? We're going to ask him to tell us the story so we can record it."

Maybe Shawn and his wife will type that story up and tape it to the back of the picture frame or keep it in a family scrapbook.

You can do this for your family. Take a walk around your house and make a list of a few fascinating objects. Write a little story about each one, and keep those stories with the object or in a special journal.

I have a vintage suitcase filled with Christmas tree ornaments that date back to the 1960s. Every ornament reflects a moment in my life or that of my extended family. I've printed out a list of the ornaments and what they mean. For instance: "This black cat ornament from 1973 represents my childhood cat, Ziggy." "This Niagara Falls ornament is from the trip with my sister and my two nieces in 2003." "This pencil ornament from 2015 represents the year my son got accepted into the Creative Writing Program at School of the Arts."

Imagine how special this will be for friends and family; it gives a deeper meaning to your belongings and connects them to your bigger storyline.

And once again, doing a project like this will help ground you in the many small joys of your lifetime. It is a reflection process that doubles as a gratitude practice!

Celebrate Your Life

No matter how you've chosen to tell your stories and share your wisdom, I encourage you not to simply set it all aside for after you are gone. Share and celebrate your stories *now*.

Gail Trunick told me she has been having so much fun sharing stories with her children and getting to see the surprise on their faces when they say, "Whaaat? I didn't know that about you!" My friend Allen got to perform his amazing musical theater piece expressing the journey of his life for dozens of his delighted friends at a small theater in San Francisco. I love to tell my son and my nieces the stories behind artwork and ornaments they made for me as little kids. Sure, I've also documented all of that. But it is so connecting to share the family history and laugh over the fun memories now.

Remember what Phil Schroeder said about our lives being a *gift*? I want you to celebrate the gift of your life—over and over. Share your interview questions and responses over dinner, and go around the table inviting each person to respond to questions like what they are most proud of or their favorite book. Let storytelling become a channel for you to express gratitude for the gift of your life and the people you love!

I promise you: Choosing any of these techniques to tell your story and share your life lessons will bring you so much unexpected joy and a depth of meaning!

Guiding Questions About Sharing My Life Stories and Wisdom

- Have I already written or recorded any of the stories of my life?

- Do I feel drawn to something very, very simple, such as responding to the eight questions on the worksheet on the next page? Or am I drawn to a more extensive set of questions, such as those the QR code links to below? In the alternative, am I interested in something like StoryWorth which will lead me through an even bigger process?

- Do I want to write a memoir, a collection of poems, a series of letters or essays?

- Am I interested in other ways to tell my life story—via music, art, scrapbooks, videos, or other creative forms?

- Do I want to create a retrospective exhibition or a legacy project as a visual artist in painting, sculpture, or photography? Do I want to self-publish a book of my art or photos?

- Do I want to produce an autobiographical film, play, or documentary?

- Do I want to choreograph and record a dance performance about my life?

- Do I want to create some kind of digital work that represents my life and story?

- Are there special objects or art in my house that are a part of my life story? Have I taken a walk around and noted them down yet? Would I want to designate a binder or scrapbook for these stories that add another layer of meaning to my narrative of my life?

☑ Section 6 Worksheet: Checklist and Fill In

❏ **I have written out my stories and wisdom.**

This book or these documents can be found _____

_____

❏ **I have left an alternative kind of creative memoir or storytelling vehicle in the form of** _____.

This alternative memoir or story can be found _____

_____

❏ **I have documented the fascinating and memorable objects around the house that add to my life story.**

The book or binder of these stories can be found _____

_____

Or I have included the story inside or on the back of these art objects or other mementos:

_____

_____

_____

_____

_____

_____

_____

_____

_____

_____

I haven't had a chance to formally write out my stories, create an alternative storytelling vehicle, or document the stories behind my art objects and mementos. However, I want you to know these things about me. (Note: a blank journal might be helpful here!)

- What I am most grateful for about my life is:

  _____

  _____

  _____

- My three biggest lessons about life or the words of wisdom I'd like to offer are:

  _____

  _____

  _____

- My top five favorite memories or memorable moments are:

  _____

  _____

  _____

- Five things I am very proud of from my life are:

  _____

  _____

  _____

- Ten people I've loved deeply are:

  _____

  _____

  _____

- My favorite gifts or words of wisdom from people I love are:

  _____

  _____

  _____

- My favorite quote is:

  _____

  _____

  _____

- My favorite vacation of my life was:

  _____

  _____

  _____

- My favorite book is:

  _____

  _____

  _____

- My favorite movie is:

  _____

  _____

  _____

- My three favorite foods are:

  _____

  _____

  _____

- Something not very many people know about me is:

  _____

  _____

  _____

True Legacy: Last Love Lists

"To live in hearts we leave behind is not to die."
—Thomas Campbell

The Love You Leave Behind

You Have So Much Love in Your Heart

Remember at the beginning of this book when I talked about "Leave not a trace"? Well, I want to add an addendum to that imperative. It is this: "Leave love behind."

We've now done everything we can to make the end of our life easier on our friends and family in terms of legal documents, clutter clearing, household itemizing, and other logistical aspects of our lives so that we know we are leaving peace and ease behind.

Now, it is time to turn our attention to the true heart of a legacy: *love*.

I read somewhere recently that one hundred years after we die, very little that is tangible remains of our lives, if anything. Think about it: What do you own that belonged to your great grandmother or grandfather, who likely died a century ago? Maybe you have a photo or two. Perhaps you have a piece of jewelry or an antique dish? Chances are that vibrant, intelligent, fascinating person has been slowly erased from the physical plane.

However, they have left the most important legacy: that which lives on in the hearts of others.

I never met my great grandmother, but I've heard stories from my mom about her. My mom's grandmother, Helen, was always gentle and loving. She sewed my mom dresses made out of flour sacks. She'd bake special donuts and dip them in cinnamon sugar as treats for my mom and her sister. She loved the garden and all the creatures in nature.

My great grandma Helen left behind a gentleness toward animals and a love of beauty that I saw in her daughter, my grandma. And that I see in my mom. And in myself.

The *love* that we live and that we are can continue on for the rest of the ages of humanity—even if it doesn't have our name on it anymore.

How do we become familiar with the love that we are? How do we prepare to leave love behind? Get ready, because I am going to share with you one of the most magical and life-changing secrets ever!

The love we see in others and that we feel for others *is* the love we are.

This Part of the Process Is Joyful and Fulfilling

So many of the preparations you've already completed will be crucial to relieving stress and anxiety for your family and friends. It is almost as if you've created a safe cocoon for your loved ones after you're gone—spaciousness for the people you love to grieve your loss without having to tackle logistical nightmares.

To return to our hiking trail metaphor, it is as if you've been building a sweet little cabin and equipping it with everything they need to be comfortable. Now, you get to move on to creating what will feel like twinkle lights, a vase of beautiful flowers, or colorful artwork inside that cabin.

I believe that this section of the book is the heart of this entire process. I'm so excited for you to embark on this part of the journey. If you do this, it will change your life and bring a lot of joy to the people you love!

Your Expressions of Love Will Live On Forever

My previous book is called *Say It Now*. The premise of that book is my life's mission: to express love and appreciation for our family and friends.

None of us know how much time we have left on this planet or how much time our loved ones have. Even if we live long, full lives, it goes by quickly. It is so important to take the time to celebrate, express, and bask in how important the people in our lives are to us.

-ׁ◌ׁ- EXPERT TIP:
Say—and Ask—It Now

"When my mom was close to death, I remember her asking me, 'Shawn, was I a good mom?' I was so shocked and surprised. Where was this coming from? Did I not tell her enough? Of course, I was grateful to be able to assure her and convey to her what an amazing mom she was and how she was always there for me. It meant a lot that I could say that to her before she passed.

It was a powerful moment between us, and it made me wonder if there were more things that were unsaid, that should have been said, that never will be now, you know?

It is such a great reminder that while we are alive, we should say all those important and meaningful things—even if we think the other person already knows it. And if we want to hear certain things, especially toward the end of our lives, it is time to be courageous enough to ask!"

—Shawn Buttner, high performance coach and podcaster

Your Expressions of Love Will Fuel *You* Right Now

When I was a young woman, I went through a very dark and difficult time of my life. I couldn't see my own worth. I didn't feel as if I had any purpose on the planet. I was tortured by negative, looping thoughts about what a mess I was and what a burden I imposed on people. I wasn't living up to my potential. The loudest looping thought was, "You should just find a way off this planet." My life was filled with anxiety and depression.

Two things happened that saved me: I was led to a meditation class where I learned to practice letting go of that tumultuous and toxic mind talk. I slowly started to feel less anxious, less self-judging, and more and more at peace.

From that place, the second thing happened that saved me. A beautiful practice bloomed out of nowhere, as if it had been planted in me and suddenly sprouted: I started making lists of reasons why I loved people in my life.

I believe this was a gift to me from the Universe. I really do. It is a form of meditation—yet so much more.

It started with my mom. When she turned fifty, I decided to write "Fifty Reasons I Love You." I was a young woman and had been so self-involved with my anxiety and depression that I had never really focused on all the beautiful aspects of my mom. Dare I say I had taken her for granted in many ways.

However, as I reflected on my childhood and young adulthood, many more things started dropping into view. My mom single-handedly raised not only her own three children, but also my cousin. She worked long hours at a hospital an hour away and never complained about having to get up so early to make that drive, work all day, then come home to make us dinner. She always left us little notes on the kitchen table: "Have a good day. Eat an apple. Be good kids." My mom loves to read, and she instilled in us a beautiful love of books; she was always taking us to visit the library or bookmobile from the time we learned to read. She took great pleasure in sitting on the porch with a cup of coffee, watching the squirrels and birds.

That list of "Fifty Reasons I Love My Mom" pretty easily turned into One Hundred Reasons! It filled me with joy and energy. I'm not exaggerating when I say that the process changed my life. Before I even put that gift in the mail, I'd deepened my relationship with my mom. I had connected to a well of love I didn't even know was inside of me.

Here's the other thing that happened: While I was focusing on all the things I loved about my mom, I replaced looping anxious thoughts with happy loving thoughts. Back then, the phrase "neural pathways" was not part of the common vernacular the way it is now. I didn't know it, but I know it now: I was literally rewiring my brain away from fear and anxiety to peacefulness and love. I was beginning to train my brain to look for the good.

I realized one of the biggest secrets in life: It is impossible to feel depressed when we are focused on love.

I'm feeling emotional as I write this because it feels so tender and poignant to relive and revisit the impact someone has had on our lives and the imprint of joy they leave on us.

I believe that *love* is energy. I believe that when I was writing that *Love List* to my mom, she could somehow feel it, even before I typed it up on my old avocado-colored electric typewriter and sent it to her. But just as importantly, as I was creating that *Love List*, I was fueling myself and literally filling my body with good energy.

❤️🔍 USEFUL TOOLS:

Create a Favorite People List

You don't need to write this all out yet, but it is super helpful to intentionally begin reflecting on the people who have had the biggest impact on your life. That way, when it comes time for the worksheets—and for creating your *Love Lists!*—the people who have mattered the most to you will be top of mind. It's kind of like priming the pump!

One of the most useful tools for this process is photographs. Set aside thirty minutes or an hour to browse through photo albums—digital or actual—from as far back as you have them. You don't have to do anything except swim around in memories. Savor all of the forgotten and important moments that were captured. (As poet Derek Walcott beautifully says, "Feast on your life.")

If you don't have many (or any) photos, an alternative tool is to take a walk in nature and simply reflect on the chapters of your life: childhood, young adulthood, college, career, marriage, hobbies. It doesn't matter how you label the chapters in your mind—or whether it's chronological or topic-based. Let yourself muse about the people who contributed to your life during each of those chapters.

One of the Most Meaningful Practices You Can Do

Having learned firsthand the real power of the *Love List* practice as a way to tap into the treasury of memories that create a legacy of love, I founded Simply Celebrate to help people express the love they feel for others.

A *Love List* is:

- a meditation practice
- a gratitude practice
- a way to rewire the brain
- a way to generate energy
- a way to relive joyful memories
- the best gift you can give someone
- a lasting legacy of love and appreciation

And you know what else I love about the *Love List*? It doesn't cost a dime. Anyone, anywhere, with a pencil and something to write on can create one. In fact, you don't even need those: You could turn on your smartphone, open up the voice recording app, and make an audio *Love List*!

You have already put a great deal of time and energy into preparing for the time you aren't here. I applaud you for all that you have done. And now, I am inviting you to the next stage of creating your legacy—leaving love behind.

Head over to the worksheets at the end of this section. I'll walk you through creating Love Lists!

-ϙ- **EXPERT TIP:**

Expressing Love and Appreciation Brings Great Peace

"I once received a random call from a former student who was about to head out to volunteer with the Peace Corps. He asked me to go for a walk with him before he started his travels. It turns out that he had made a list of everyone he wanted to say thank you to before he left the country. I was on the list!

As we walked, Dan shared ways I'd influenced his life and how much he appreciated me. I was deeply touched by his words, and curious about this list he had made. A month later, Dan called me to report that he had just checked the last person off his list. 'How did it feel?' I asked. 'I have a sense of peace that I have never felt before,' he replied. 'I've said everything I wanted to say to everyone I know.'

Flash forward fifteen years: I remembered Dan and his list, and I thought, 'I want to make one of my own.' So, I made a list of forty-two people I'd want to thank before I died. I wrote out a card each day, and after forty-two days, I dropped them in the mail.

It was a deeply satisfying experience. It turns out Dan was right. Writing those letters brought me a profound sense of peace. If I found out tomorrow that I had terminal cancer, I wouldn't have much unfinished business to tend to. Writing those letters felt complete and so good.

This is something everyone should think about doing."

—Paul Wesselmann, The Ripples Guy

I agree 100 percent about feeling more peace when we express our love and gratitude to people in our lives. You can write letters, certainly. However, I want you to consider making your gratitude letters in the form of *Love Lists*. The list format will make it feel simpler and will give you room for memories, humor, and your wishes for that person. I can't wait for you to try it!

Time for You to Celebrate Yourself!

You are amazing. Don't leave yourself out of all this love! One of the most wonderful things we can do is create a *Love List* selfie. Yep, just like when you hold the phone up to take your own photo, making a *Love List* for yourself is like holding up a metaphorical mirror so you can see all of the wonderful and loving things about yourself. It's okay if it feels a little uncomfortable. Trust me—you deserve the happy impact it is sure to have on you once you do it.

Click this QR code to download the *Love List* Tool
Kit, tips on your *Love List* selfie, and more!

⟨?⟩ Section 7 Worksheet: Guiding Questions

Questions to Ask Myself About the People in My Life

- Who are my family members (immediate and extended relatives) whom I want to leave a boost of love?

- Who are my friends (close companions from various stages of life) whom I want to leave a boost of love?

- Who are my coworkers (colleagues from past and present jobs) whom I want to leave a boost of love?

- Who are my teachers (educators and instructors from school, college, or other learning environments) whom I want to leave a boost of love?

- Who are my fellow hobby enthusiasts (people I know from shared interests like sports, arts, or crafts) whom I want to leave a boost of love?

- Who are my fellow club members (individuals I've met through clubs, organizations, or associations) whom I want to leave a boost of love?

- Who are the authors, artists, or musicians (creators whose work has influenced or inspired me) whom I want to leave a boost of love?

- Who are my neighbors (people who live or have lived near me) whom I want to leave a boost of love?

- Who are my health care providers (doctors, nurses, and other professionals who have cared for me) whom I want to leave a boost of love?

- Who are my community members (acquaintances from my local area, religious groups, or volunteer work) whom I want to leave a boost of love?

- Who are my classmates (people with whom I attended school or took courses) whom I want to leave a boost of love?

- Who are my mentors (individuals who have offered guidance or advice) whom I want to leave a boost of love?

- Who are my online connections (friends or contacts made through social media, online communities, or gaming) whom I want to leave a boost of love?

- Who are my service providers (regular contacts like hairstylists, mechanics, or other local business owners) whom I want to leave a boost of love?

- Who are my travel companions (people I've met or traveled with during trips or vacations) whom I want to leave a boost of love?

Questions to Ask Myself About the Format and Delivery of *Love Lists* I Write

- **Do I want to type my *Love Lists* or handwrite them?**

   (Handwriting might feel more personal, while typing could be more practical for longer lists.)

- **Do I want to give a copy to each person now while I'm alive, or should I arrange for them to be a surprise after I'm gone?**

   (Consider the impact of each option on both you and the recipient.)

- **Should I buy special paper, cards, or stationery to make these àlists feel extra special?**

   (Think about whether the physical presentation adds to the sentiment you want to convey.)

- **Do I want to include photos, mementos, or small gifts with the lists?**

   (These could add a meaningful touch, especially for shared memories.)

- **Should I personalize each list with unique touches, or would I prefer a consistent format across all lists?**

   (Consistency can create a theme, but personalization can make each list feel uniquely special.)

- **Do I want to write these lists all at once or spread them out over time?**

  (Consider whether this is a project you want to complete in a focused effort or as an ongoing practice.)

- **Would I prefer to keep a copy of each list for myself as a keepsake, or should the recipient be the sole owner?**

  (Keeping a copy could serve as a meaningful record of your relationships.)

- **How do I want to address and sign each list?**

  (The way you sign off—whether with a simple name, a nickname, or a heartfelt phrase—can leave a lasting impression.)

- **Do I want to include a specific date on each list, or should they remain timeless?**

  (Dating the lists could add significance, particularly if the date is related to a special occasion.)

- **Should I plan a special event or moment to present the lists, or simply give them as I feel inspired?**

  (A planned presentation could create a memorable experience, but spontaneous giving can feel more natural.)

- **Do I want to keep adding to my lists over time?**

  (This approach allows you to capture new memories and thoughts as your relationships evolve.)

- **Do I want to create an audio or video list instead of writing it?**

  (An audio or video message can capture tone, emotion, and expression in a way that words on a page might not.)

☑ Section 7 Worksheet: Checklist and Fill In

My Favorite People List

These are the people for whom I definitely want to create *Love Lists* and either give them now and/or leave them as a surprise for after I pass.

_____

_____

_____

_____

_____

_____

Love List Prompts

You can try your hand at writing a *Love List* directly in this book. Think of one person you love and respond next to any of the prompts below that resonate with you for this person. See how wonderful it feels and then write or type some more, outside of this book, based on the "Favorite People" list you created.

This *Love List* is for_____

- What is a tiny thing they do that brings you joy?
  (*Example: "I love the way you always send me handwritten notes on special occasions."*)

  _____

- What quirky habits or preferences do they have that you find endearing?
  (*Example: "I love that you insist on having pickles with every meal."*)

  _____

- How do they interact with others in a way that makes you proud or happy?
  (*Example: "I love how you always go out of your way to make strangers feel welcome."*)

  _____

The Love List of a Lifetime

- What is a memorable moment you've shared that you treasure?
  (*Example: "I love that time we got lost in the city and ended up discovering a hidden café together."*)

  _____

- What is a gift or words of wisdom they've given you that you cherish?
  (*Example: "I love that you once told me, 'Always be kind, even when it's hard,' and I've carried that with me ever since."*)

  _____

- What is something you regularly do together that makes your relationship special?
  (*Example: "I love that you're my partner for spontaneous weekend road trips."*)

  _____

- What is a physical trait or item they wear that you love?
  (*Example: "I love your old, worn-out baseball cap that you refuse to replace."*)

  _____

- What is something special captured in a photograph that represents them well?
  (*Example: "I love that picture of you laughing uncontrollably at the beach."*)

  _____

- How did you meet, and what makes that moment special?
  (*Example: "I love that we met at that random bookstore event—it was so unexpected yet perfect."*)

  _____

- What is a childhood memory or quirk that makes you smile?
  (*Example: "I love that you used to call butterflies 'flutterbys' when you were little."*)

  _____

- What unique trait or characteristic do they have that you admire?
  (*Example: "I love your ability to stay calm and optimistic even in tough situations."*)

  _____

To My Next of Kin

Below you will find a list of people to whom I have written about my appreciation and love. I have written my *Love Lists* or loving notes, put them in envelopes, and addressed them with current mailing addresses. Could you kindly stamp and mail them for me?

Send my letters to the following recipients:

_____

_____

_____

_____

_____

_____

_____

_____

_____

These letters can be found here: _____

SECTION 8

There's Still Time

"Carpe diem. Seize the day, boys. Make your lives extraordinary."
—Robin Williams in *Dead Poets Society*

As Long as We Are Alive, We Can Connect, Grow, and Change

You Are Still Here and There's Still Time

No matter what age you are when you are reading this book, you still have the chance to make a big difference in your own life and in the lives of the people you love most. You are *here*! You are alive! And that means that there is still time to focus on what matters most. That means you have time to live the life you've always wanted to live.

I'm so proud of you for everything you've accomplished thus far and for sticking with this journey. I'm proud of you for doing hard things. I'm proud of you for loving the people in your life so well that you are willing to do many challenging things to ease their future pain and frustration.

This last section may seem like it is focused mainly on you. It is a lot about your experience of your life and how to deepen the joy of living while there is still time.

However, I remind you that no man (or woman, or anyone) is an island. Who we are and how we live our lives always impacts people around us. Everything you do to focus on presence, joy, and health is sure to have a positive effect on those around you. Here's a big spoiler alert for this section—each of those things you do that is seemingly "for yourself" is creating a beautiful legacy of love!

You Can Feel More of Everything You Want Before You Leave This Planet: There's Still Time!

Remember at the start of this book when I said, "Talking about death brings me to life?" Any moment when I remember that everything is here for such a short time is a reminder to be present and to appreciate it.

When I say that talking about death brings me to life, what I mean is that it reminds me of how impermanent absolutely everything is: my body, my beliefs, my belongings. Also, all of the people I love. The Japanese maple outside my studio window. That sweet bird chirping in the early morning hours. The coral-colored hibiscus blooming on the deck. This storm. That applause.

If that sounds trite, I get it. It is a cliché, like the old "blink and your children grow up," or "grains of sand slipping through an hourglass." But as I always tell my son, "There is a reason things become clichés—it's because there is usually some universal truth to them."

Our lives do go by quickly. It is extraordinary to be a human being on this planet. It is easy to forget how fleeting and wondrous it all is. When we take the time to pause, like you are doing right now, it can jump-start a process of taking stock: Am I living the life I most want to live? Am I loving as best I can? Am I choosing activities and people that align with my values and dreams?

The final process you are embarking on of planning for the end of our lives can have a surprising and deeply valuable impact of helping us live our lives with greater joy and celebration than we've ever experienced before.

I really believe that when we remember the possibility of loss, it fuels us to live and love fully. That's what I want for you.

As we close out this legacy planner, I encourage you to think about these last eight steps—these encouraged activities—as a celebration of life. This is *your* one and only life, and you are still here to make the most of it. Celebrate every aspect!

Choosing Wisely

There's an amazing book I encourage you to read called *Essentialism: The Disciplined Pursuit of Less*. The author, Greg McKeown, writes: "As you continue to clear out the closet of your life, you will experience a reordering of what really matters. Life will become less about efficiently crossing off what was on your to-do list or rushing through everything on your schedule and more about changing what you put on there in the first place."

It's no secret that our time is limited. It doesn't matter if you are twenty-five or eighty-five, it is essential to face that fact with courage and intention. What means the most to you? What brings you the most fulfillment? What will you give back to the world? Do those things. Put those things on your schedule!

Out of all of the possibilities for where we can focus in life, I've narrowed it down to eight essential areas.

The eight areas I've highlighted below point to places in your life where you can put your focus to make significant positive impacts on the quality of your life, your health, and your relationships. When you choose to take action in these areas, you will feel yourself grow. It is also likely you'll experience more meaning and fulfillment by doing so.

You are here. There is still time!

1. There's Still Time to Be Grateful and to Feel Fulfilled

Saying Goodbye to Regret

If we follow McKeown's guidance from the previous page, if we spend time reassessing what is on our calendars and what fills our day, there's a great chance that intentional reflection will lead to a deeper fulfillment.

I've been talking to my friend and fellow coach Morgan Oaks about how avoiding the topic of death can lead to unconscious feelings of lack and regret—the opposite of gratitude. Morgan says, "There's a billion-dollar-a-year cosmetic industry to encourage us to avoid realizing that we're actually aging. What would it look like to age gracefully? What would it look like to let go of being the twenty-something we were and step into being the fifty-, sixty-, seventy-, or eighty-year-old we are? Anytime we're grasping for what was or resisting what is going to be, we're in a place of pain and suffering. How do we really embrace where we are and make the most of that?"

It doesn't matter what your age is. What matters is your experience of your life at this moment. Will you let yourself be who you are right now, in this moment—allowing yourself to be the age that you are? Can you practice letting go of any regret over any age of your life, knowing *that* time has passed?

All you have is this moment. Please don't waste a moment of *now* on regret over anything that happened years ago or even yesterday.

In Bronnie Ware's book, *The Top Five Regrets of the Dying*, she shares that people's number one regret is, "I wish I'd had the courage to live a life true to myself, not the life others expected of me."

Even if you spent the first eighty years of your life doing what was expected of you instead of what felt true to you, it isn't too late to turn that ship around.

What does that mean to you? What is a life that is true to *yourself*? What is the first step?

Choosing to Live Meaningfully Now

I love the expression, "Your favorite glass is already broken," from a teaching by the Thai Buddhist monk Ajahn Chah Subhaddo. He used the metaphor of the broken glass to remind us about impermanence and acceptance.

Apparently, Ajahn Chah would hold up a glass and say, "You see this glass? For me, this glass is already broken. I enjoy it; I drink out of it. When the wind knocks it over or my elbow brushes it off the table and it falls to the ground and shatters, I say, 'Of course.' When I understand that the glass is already broken, every moment with it is precious."

This is the same with our lives and everything we love. When we remember that everything will be lost to us eventually, we can appreciate them more fully in the moment.

I'm inviting you to practice the deepest appreciation that comes from knowing everything in our life "is already broken." Everything you have will be lost to you one day. Let that be the meditation bell that wakes you up to fully loving what is in your hands right now.

-ᗢ- EXPERT TIP:
Focus on Meaning and What Matters

"It's helpful for us to acknowledge that talking about serious illness or death opens up the possibility of conversations with people we love that are intimate and that cut through all the noise and all the distractions. It's where we can connect deeply with people we really care about.

It also connects us to ourselves in new ways. When we think about what we might want at the end of our lives or what we want to leave behind, it puts us in conversation with ourselves about what is meaningful and what matters most. 'What inspires me? What brings me alive? What's my gift to offer the world?' Talking about our mortality helps us think about legacy."

—Roy Remer, executive director of Zen Caregiving Project

2. There's Still Time for Deeper, More Loving Relationships

Expressing Love

In the last section, I encouraged you to write *Love Lists*, or loving letters to people in your life. Did you complete that task? Expressing why we love them is one of the most important things we can ever do to feel love and connection for people in our life.

As much as possible, I want you to remember the phrase, "Say it now." If you are with your granddaughter and feeling proud of how kind she is, don't wait: Say it now. If you are laughing with your best friend of thirty years and feeling deeply grateful for his wisdom and kindness, don't wait; say it now. If you are in the market and the grocer gives you a warm smile that lights up the day and makes you thankful, don't wait, say it now.

Please don't be afraid to say it now—or you might regret it later. When we express gratitude, love, and joy, it triples! First we feel it, which is marvelous. Then the other person gets to hear it, and they feel good. Thirdly, we get the added benefit of hearing ourselves say it out loud, and we experience the joyous vibration and reverberation in our bodies.

🔍 USEFUL TOOLS:

Interview People You Love

One of the best ways to express our love and to feel an increased appreciation for people is to spend time deeply listening to their stories and to what matters most to them.

In Section 6, I mentioned an organization called StoryCorps. If you haven't had the chance to use their resources yet, there's still time! Their website has lots of support for self-directed recordings you can make. Sometimes, they even have a mobile recording studio that you can visit with a loved one to make an interview recording! You can print out the interview questions we gave you via the QR code in Section 6. Visit Storycorps.org to find out more. Not only will the interviews connect you more deeply to people in the moment, they make beautiful additions to your family's history and for your digital memory archives!

Making Amends

If there are people who were really important to you from whom you are estranged or that you have lost along the way, consider seeking them out. This is the best time to let bygones be bygones and remember what is most important. Consider asking for or offering forgiveness where necessary.

One of the most famous characters in literature is a guy named Scrooge, whose role is front and center in Charles Dickens' *A Christmas Carol*.

Thinking about his death—or rather, being forced to experience it in advance!—led him to see that he'd neglected to love the people in his life. He'd been more miserly and miserable than you ever could be. But even for that awful guy, there was still time for change, right? If he could turn things around, so can you!

Surprise People with Gifts of Shared Memories

I've always been a big fan of surprising people by printing out photographs or paper keepsakes and mailing them in greeting cards along with a line or two about the special memory.

If you've spent time organizing your memorabilia and photos (back in Sections 4 and 6), now's the time to put them to use. It is so easy to upload a digital photo to your local Walgreens or Staples and print it out for just pennies. If you have a printer at home, it is even easier!

Make it a habit to send one or two cards every week—for birthdays, anniversaries, or just because. So few people send things through postal mail anymore that they really stand out. Imagine opening your mailbox to find a handwritten greeting card and a photo memory! Pure joy, right? Do this for people. Just as with almost every other kind of gift, sending a shared memory and personal greeting will sweeten your life before it even reaches *them*!

Making Memorable Moments

Remember in Section 6 when I asked you to think about memorable moments of your life? Well, have you ever thought about what it is that makes some moments unforgettable? It may be slightly different for everyone, but I have a hunch there are some things in common that make moments stand out:

- **Novelty:** Experiencing something new or different from the usual routine.

- **Surprise:** Unexpected events or outcomes that catch us off guard.

- **Thoughtfulness:** Moments marked by care, consideration, or kindness from others.

- **Overcoming Challenge:** Achieving success in the face of difficulties or obstacles.

- **Connection:** Deep emotional or social bonds with others, nature, or oneself.

- **Emotion:** Intense feelings, whether joy, sadness, love, or fear, that leave a lasting imprint.

- **Anniversaries or Milestones:** Significant life events or achievements, such as major transitions or first experiences.

- **Sensory Impact:** Strong engagement of the senses, like a beautiful view, a memorable meal, or a distinctive smell.

- **Meaning and Purpose:** Moments that resonate with our values or give us a sense of fulfillment or purpose.

Let's say that you have time scheduled with your best friend next Thursday. Maybe you are going to your favorite Italian restaurant. How could you incorporate some of those things from the list above to make your time together go from "that's fine" to "that's unforgettable!?"

Here are a few thoughts for you. You could create an anniversary and make a big to-do. Maybe you've been friends for twenty years but don't recall the exact date. That's okay. You just claim it. You make next Thursday your "Twentieth Friendiversary," and you bring a card that you made with side-by-side photos of the two of you twenty years ago and your most recent one.

What if you told your friend you were having a special surprise celebration and to wear her most fun outfit and you would too? What if you pulled out the *Love List* you made for this friend (in the last section!) and you read it out loud to her after dinner? What if you called ahead to the restaurant and asked them to please bring your friend a piece of tiramisu after dinner with a candle in it? What if you made your friend a playlist of music that was a "Walk Down Memory Lane" of your friendship and you listened to it after dinner as you took a walk?

You know what the number one ingredient for a memorable moment is? Intention. I bet if you spend just five or ten minutes thinking about the person you want to wow, at least one or two wonderful, wow-able things will drop into your mind that you can do!

☀ EXPERT TIP:
Host a Celebration of Life

One of the best ways to acknowledge and celebrate the people who have made a difference in your life is to invite them to celebrate *you*. Yep, you can host a "Celebration of Life" or "Going Away Party" or "Life is Good Party." It doesn't matter what you call it, and it doesn't even matter if you include any formal, planned-in-advance speeches from people.

You can open up a space, bring some varied and festive foods and music, and invite everyone to celebrate the good life you have lived. Heck, if it makes you uncomfortable to have people saying all the good stuff about you, you could turn the tables and prepare something loving to point out about each of your guests.

There's something incredibly special about gathering a collection of people you've loved together. Most of us have done it for college graduation or our weddings, but we haven't done it since then.

I just heard this story recently and it underscored the joy of gathering everyone together again:

"My grandma was about ninety years old when she sold the house she'd lived in most of her life and moved closer to where my mom and I lived. Before she left, she hosted a big going-away party. She got to connect with a lot of people she had known all of her life. I'm pretty sure she planned it that way—having a chance to be with everyone while she was still alive to enjoy them, instead of all of those people attending her funeral. Wow, what if we could all have that?"

—Michelle Huljev, life coach

3. There's Still Time for Our Health and Well-Being

Care for Our Strength and Mobility

If we want to have the best chance at a happy last chapter, we have to take the best possible care of ourselves now. Mobility, strength, flexibility, and balance are hugely important as we age.

I recently turned sixty, and that means I'm turning my attention to health in a new way. I've been reading about how to best care for my body as I age: the benefits of strength training, as well as exercises for bone, joint, and heart health, increased cardio, and much more.

Last week, my twenty-four-year-old son, Kayne, offered me an hour-long kettlebell training so I could increase my muscle strength while also contributing to bone health. I've also found some new Zumba classes to attend, two of which are outdoors, which help mobility and provide fresh air and sunshine to this gal who works on a computer most of the day. I'm also practicing stacking habits by standing on one foot while I brush my teeth or wait for the tea water to boil. Your health habits may look different from mine. The important thing is, are you being intentional about maintaining your mobility, flexibility, and strength so you can continue to age with joy?

Focus on Your Emotional Health

Almost all of the suggestions in this section of the book are great for your emotional health. You don't have to do them all, but please appreciate yourself for any that you spend time on.

Too many people forget that we can strengthen our mental and emotional health every day we are walking on this planet! What can you do today to feel more grounded, centered, and emotionally connected to your life?

4. There's Still Time to Connect to the Great Sumpthin' Sumpthin'

Regardless of what faith or religion you are—including agnostic, nihilist, or materialist—now's the time to get crystal clear with yourself and know that you are aligned with your beliefs, whatever they are.

If you have spiritual practices, perhaps go deeper now. If you don't follow any organized religion, philosophy, or spiritual practices, take time to reflect on what matters to you outside of yourself.

So many people don't want to think about the fact that life is finite. But there is an end coming, isn't that right—for all of us, no matter what age we are.

In a conversation I had recently with psychologist Dr. Douglas Anderson, I reminded him that during the times we'd talked over the last few years, he'd repeatedly said, "I'm aging," and "I'm looking at that. There's a lot to learn from it." I'd been impressed with how obviously mindful he was about aging as a part of spiritual practice.

So I asked him if he could share some compassionate words for people on how to make aging and dying feel less morbid and scary—and a bit more meaningful and mindful. He said:

> We need to talk about this because it's coming. It's coming like a train straight down the track, and there's no avoiding it. It's the one thing we all share. It's *the* great mystery. Those are the qualities that make it so amazing to dive into, explore, and prepare for.
>
> It helps to have some kind of awareness practice, some way of looking at and being with it. Buddhism is great that way. The Buddha himself started his journey when he saw sickness, old age, and death. That's what woke him up.

I encourage you to find support for waking up in your own ways to greater understanding and acceptance of the impermanence of life. Reach out to a church elder, spiritual teacher, or trusted friend to discuss this.

-☼- **EXPERT TIP:**

Explore Your Ancestry and Spiritual Roots

"I think we can all lean into our ancestry more when
it comes to thinking about death.

Americans tend to not be good at this. Consider the Mexican tradition around
the Day of the Dead. They put up altars for their deceased and celebrate
them every year. They have a fun relationship with death—skeletons getting
married, dancing, and so on. They celebrate death rather than resisting it.

A simple online search may uncover traditions that your ancestors practiced
that you have never experienced with your family. What rituals from your
family line can support you in your grieving, or with your own passing?

Leaning into these traditions helps us get into alignment before we need
them. Many people also believe that our ancestors (and/or spiritual figures
from our traditions) will help us cross over when the time comes."

—Dr. Morgan Oaks, chiropractor, high performance coach, and transformational speaker

5. There's Still Time for Discovery and Adventure

Growing, Learning, and Skilling Up

No matter what your age, it's possible to continue to grow and thrive.

I volunteer at a nursing home in San Francisco, and on Sundays, they need assistance helping people in wheelchairs to get downstairs for an afternoon concert. Last weekend, I went to pick up a man named John from his room to wheel him to the concert. He had several guitars hanging on the walls, and he also had a keyboard in his room. I said, "Wow, are you a musician?" He said, "Not yet. I am learning how to play the guitar, and I also want to learn how to play piano. However, I'm in the middle of writing a book, and so I may have to wait to learn piano."

I was inspired by him! I love people who are lifelong learners. I could feel his enthusiasm and energy. He is living his last years at a nursing home, making the most of what he is able to do: create and learn and connect with others!

Are there things you've always wanted to learn? Will you hop on YouTube or sign up for lessons? Have fun learning!

☀ EXPERT TIP:
Now's the Time to Live with Greater Intention and Purpose

"Planning for the end of life is not just a practical task but a profoundly transformative experience that can spur significant personal growth. By confronting the reality of mortality—I call it 'Mortality Motivation'—we're compelled to evaluate what's truly important, prioritize our deepest values, and live with greater intention, urgency, and purpose. This process of reflection can lead to a deeper appreciation of life and a clearer understanding of how we want to spend our time and energy. It's about making the most of every day, knowing that each one is a nonrenewable resource. It's a powerful catalyst to live fully, to cherish each breath, and to make your life a bold and beautiful adventure."

—Brendon Burchard, *New York Times* bestselling author and world-renowned high performance coach

Making a Bucket List

Many of us know the expression "bucket list," and we understand that it is typically defined as a collection of goals, dreams, or experiences that someone wants to achieve or do during their lifetime.

However, I bet that most of us have forgotten where that expression comes from. The term "bucket list" comes from the cavalier phrase "kick the bucket," meaning to die. So, when we're making our bucket list, it typically includes things we want to do before we die.

I'm reminding us of all of this because I think it is really important to have things that we aspire to and are anticipating. Goals and future adventures can give us a lot of joy—not just when we accomplish them, but in planning for them and the energy of working to reach them.

What future experiences are pulling you into the future? What are you looking forward to, and with whom?

I have a good friend who told me that even before he moves away from a town, he thinks about which nature hikes, experiences, or people he still wants to see or experience. "It's a smaller version of thinking about what to do before dying," he said.

6. There's Still Time to Tie Up Loose Ends

Dotting the Is and Crossing the Ts

This planner is chock-full of so many aspects of our lives to set in order—legally and logistically. Now's the time to check and see if you missed anything in the process.

You can look through the worksheets at the end of every section. Are there things you said you'd come back to, but haven't yet?

Make a list and check 'em off, okay? Remember, every step you take relieves someone you love of a challenge or frustration down the road.

You've got this!

☀ EXPERT TIP:
Double Check Your Work

I know you have put a lot of time, effort, and thought into getting all of your legal documents and household affairs in order.

Don't forget to review all of your documents every few years, just to make sure that you haven't changed your mind about anything or to check to see if new situations in your life might require changes.

Here's a good reminder about why this is so important:

> **"Make sure you review your legal documents every few years, especially if you move! My husband and I had everything done legally in California, then we moved to Hawaii. When hospice came, they asked if we had a 'Do Not Resuscitate' document. I said yes and handed them the document, but they said it wouldn't work in Hawaii. Even though it was a legal document, they explained that Hawaii requires a green sheet of paper with specific information, and that it must be placed on the refrigerator so an ambulance can see it immediately."**

—Emily Thiroux Threatt, founder of Grief and Happiness Alliance, author, and podcast host

That's a great example of how laws differ depending where we live. I'm grateful for Emily's story.

I also appreciate that she added, "I didn't really want that hanging on my refrigerator where I would see it every time I walked by, but that's what they want people to do!"

It gave me pause to think: maybe it wouldn't be so bad to have a reminder of the end of life right there on my fridge. Maybe every time I saw it, I would think: "I'm not always going to be here. I should call my mom today! I will text my son! How can I live more fully now?"

7. There's Still Time to Leave a Loving Legacy—in Each and Every Moment You Have

Bringing Kindness and Compassion into This Moment Now

I learned a beautiful concept from Mel Abraham, a colleague at GrowthDay, where I work.

Mel said, "I don't believe legacy is created at death. I believe legacy is created within the moment. Every moment we have that we can impact someone's life is a moment that creates legacy, because that person is forever changed. These moments, as simple as a kind word or gesture, can change the direction of someone's life, creating a lasting impact."

Mel is a CPA and author of the book *Building Your Money Machine*, so he is well-versed in how to leave a financial legacy and ease that burden on your next of kin. However, Mel helps us recognize that kindness and generosity in the moment not only make a huge difference, they are essential elements of our legacy.

He added, "When you realize that each moment has the power to change and create legacy, I think we then give each moment the presence and reverence it deserves. There are no inconsequential moments."

I still remember singular moments when I was going through hard times and a stranger would say hello to me or offer a smile. Those acts of kindness live on in me and ripple out. Maybe those folks don't know it, but that kindness is part of their legacy.

It doesn't matter if you are 101 years old when you are reading this passage. You have this moment now to intentionally create legacy by offering kindness to someone you love or to a stranger you pass.

8. There's Still Time to Experience Countless Moments of Simple Joy

Joy Is Around the Corner If We Allow It

One of the best things we can do for ourselves and everyone around us is to invite in more joyful moments.

Our planet is filled with so much hardship and challenges. Aging and change can be difficult; yet amidst all of that, there is great joy and delight waiting for us. It is essential that we pay attention and that we seek it out.

There's a powerful podcast episode in which *Essentialism* author Greg McKeown is in conversation with his best friend of many decades, Sam Bridgstock. Sam has a terminal illness and has been given less than a year to live.

How do we grapple with the actual end of our beautiful lives? Especially when, as Sam says, "So much of our optimism and joy comes from thinking about the future—the next holiday, when we'll retire, what the next job might look like, or the next new house. The ability to dream is a very strong thing."

In that conversation, Sam talks about having to manage the difficult emotions around every new social invitation. "I was told I will not live beyond twelve months. At some point I'm going to dip and will be in more pain. So with every invitation, I think, 'Will I be going to that?' No one else is thinking that. Everyone's thinking, 'Oh, that's great; it's a party or a nice social gathering, or we're all going on holiday.' I've noticed that it's destroyed lots of peace for me."

Sam goes on to muse about the last few years and his illness and all the joy he has experienced despite being sick. He intentionally flips his thoughts back to a deep place of peace.

Sam shares this beautiful thought with us:

> I think that for all of us, wherever we are, however bleak now may look, or how uncertain the future may be, I'm telling you, life will offer you a chance to be joyful tomorrow if you take it.
>
> That may be waking up and looking at the sky and seeing it's still blue and beautiful. It might be a lovely meal with a child, or maybe laughter with someone, or seeing a friend that you've missed.
>
> Every day those moments come for me.

And those moments are waiting for *you*, too.

It is our important work to hold onto the faith that beautiful moments are around the corner. If you look, I know you will find them and feel uplifted by them.

Scan Me

Listen to the entire powerful conversation between Sam and Greg McKeown: "Essential Trade-offs and Saying Yes with Sam Bridgstock (Part 1 + Part 2)," *The Greg McKeown Podcast*

Seeking and Creating Pinpricks of Light

One of the biggest gifts I received from overcoming depression and anxiety as a young woman was a simple yet powerful tool that helps me find tiny moments of joy.

In the darkest moment of my life, I was led to a meditation class via a book by Zen teacher Cheri Huber. When I walked into that meditation group, I was feeling as if the depression was a thick iron wall closing in on me. The sensation was solid and constant.

During one of the instructions to "breathe in and breathe out," when we were asked to focus completely on our breath, something happened. I felt a moment of profound well-being. I was free for just a moment. It was amazing.

All the sadness and anxiety came rushing back in. However, that one tiny moment was like a pinprick of light in the iron wall. And you know how, when you have the experience of being in the pitch dark, the tiniest bit of light can feel like a lighthouse beacon? That's what that moment was for me.

It showed me that feelings aren't constant and unyielding, like I had thought. It was an experience of what was possible.

If I could have that singular moment of freedom and well-being within the darkest feelings, then I knew I could have another. I began practicing looking for tiny moments of well-being or joy: pinpricks of light.

When I was holding my cat and feeling her purr, I was okay. When I tasted the blueberry jam on my toast, I was okay. When I noticed the way the sun slanted in through the window, I was okay.

As time went by, I learned to not only seek these moments of well-being, but to *create* them. I trained my brain to look for ways to feel pinpricks of light. If I was super sad, I would call my mom and focus on the sound of her loving voice. I would go to the ocean and feel the warm sand under my bare feet. I would bask in the sound of the street musician's accordion.

With every pinprick of light in that heavy iron wall, my life felt that much brighter.

When we are scared, sad, exhausted, or hopeless, we can practice seeking and creating pinpricks of light as if they are stepping stones to help us survive the hard moments.

I encourage you to use this practice to find moments of joy.

You don't even have to be feeling upset, anxious, or hopeless to try it. You can use it anytime you simply want a boost of well-being!

Give yourself the gift of feeling more joy.

Your joy is also a gift to everyone in your life. It is one of the most treasured aspects of your legacy.

Celebration

Wow. I hope that as you've been considering all of these areas where you still have time, that has felt like a gift. I hope this section of the book has shown you that your energy and breath are fuel for creativity and change. The truth is, every day we are alive is a gift. It's easy to forget that, but the more we remind ourselves, the more we feel it.

You know what else is a gift? *You.* Each of these things you seemingly do "for yourself" is lighting the path for someone in your life who is watching. Each action you take to care for yourself and to be intentional about your life is providing a role model for someone you love to do the same.

I've invited you to celebrate at the end of every section we've covered together in this book. This celebration is especially important.

You have completed every aspect of end-of-life planning! You've done it!

Now, there is just one last thing to do: *Celebrate.* Please don't skip this essential part of the process.

Here are three things you can do. Choose one or do all three!

- Invite someone (or several someones) close to you to share a meal in your favorite restaurant. Raise a glass and toast that person or people. Tell them about this process, and let them know it was a labor of love on their behalf because they matter to you.

- Take a walk in your favorite place in nature—a forest, a meadow, by the ocean. Bring a picnic of various yummy foods. Also bring a journal, sketchbook, or your smartphone. Write, draw, or audio record a loving message to yourself. Express gratitude in a way that feels right and good to you.

- Take a look at the bucket list you created earlier in this section and choose one thing on it. *Plan it.* Put it on your calendar and take the first steps toward making it happen. Keep that promise to yourself.

Today is a special occasion. It's called your life. Don't wait; celebrate now.

Scan Me

The very first time I met with Brenda Knight, my wonderful editor for this book, she played me the song "Little Black Train" by the Carter Family, from the album *In the Shadow of Clinch Mountain*. It made me smile wide. Go find it on YouTube and give it a listen as you celebrate how you've "set your business right"!

[?] Section 8 Worksheet: Guiding Questions

Questions to Ask Myself About Gratitude and Fulfillment

- Have I let go of any regrets that may be holding me back from feeling at peace with my life?

- Am I finding meaning and purpose in the life I have lived, accepting and appreciating it for what it has been?

- Am I embracing a sense of gratitude for my experiences, both the joys and the challenges, and feeling fulfilled by the journey?

Questions to Ask Myself About My Relationships

- Am I nurturing and strengthening my connections with family, friends, and loved ones?

- Am I spending quality time with those close to me, expressing gratitude, and resolving any lingering issues?

- Have I worked on healing relationships by seeking or offering forgiveness, making amends, and resolving any conflicts or regrets?

Questions to Ask Myself About My Health

- Am I prioritizing my physical well-being by managing any health conditions, maintaining a healthy lifestyle, and addressing any medical issues?

- Have I explored alternative therapies or wellness practices that bring comfort and peace?

The Love List of a Lifetime

Questions to Ask Myself About My Spirituality

- Am I deepening my spiritual practice, whether through meditation, prayer, reflection, or connecting with a faith community?

- If I don't have a faith or belief, how am I connecting to something outside of myself?

- Have I explored what brings me peace, comfort, and a sense of purpose or connection to something greater than myself?

Questions to Ask Myself About Discovery and Adventure

- Am I embracing the spirit of adventure by pursuing experiences that bring joy, excitement, or fulfillment?

- Am I engaging in creative pursuits that allow me to express my thoughts, emotions, and experiences?

- Am I continuing to grow intellectually and emotionally by exploring new ideas, taking up hobbies, or engaging in stimulating activities?

Questions to Ask Myself About Tying Up Loose Ends

- Have I double-checked that all my legal documents, such as my will, power of attorney, and health care directives, are up to date and reflect my current wishes?

- Have I ensured that my financial accounts, including beneficiaries and access details, are in order and clearly documented?

- Have I reviewed and organized all my end-of-life plans, including funeral arrangements, so that my loved ones have clear guidance?

- Have I communicated where all of my important documents and information are stored so my loved ones can easily access them when needed?

- Is everything my loved ones need in a Nokbox or my own file box?

Questions to Ask Myself About Legacy and Impact

- Have I considered the legacy I want to leave behind?

- Have I been documenting my life stories, writing letters to loved ones, or making contributions to causes I care about?

- How do I see myself making my legacy every moment?

Questions to Ask Myself About Joy and Presence

- Am I focusing on being present in the moment and finding joy in simple things?

- Am I practicing mindfulness and savoring everyday pleasures to bring a deeper sense of contentment and fulfillment?

- Am I allowing myself to experience greater connection to life by being present for simple and daily joys?

- What do I want to do to celebrate myself for completing this process?

✅ Section 8 Worksheet: Checklist and Fill In

1. GRATITUDE AND FULFILLMENT: LETTING GO AND FINDING MEANING

Letting Go of Regrets:

❑ Have I let go of any regrets that may be holding me back from feeling at peace with my life?

The regrets I need to acknowledge and release are: _____

_____

The steps I can take to let go of these regrets include: _____

_____

The sense of peace I hope to achieve by releasing these regrets is: _____

_____

Finding Meaning in My Life:

❑ Am I finding meaning and purpose in the life I have lived, accepting and appreciating it for what it has been?

The meaningful experiences or moments I want to reflect on include: _____

_____

The lessons or insights I have gained from these experiences are: _____

_____

The way I can embrace and appreciate my journey is: _____

_____

Embracing Gratitude and Fulfillment:

❑ Am I embracing a sense of gratitude for my experiences, both the joys and the challenges, and feeling fulfilled by the journey?

The experiences I am grateful for include: _____

The challenges that have helped me grow are: _____

_____

The sense of fulfillment I feel by acknowledging my journey is: _____

_____

2. RELATIONSHIPS: NURTURING AND STRENGTHENING CONNECTIONS

❏ **Am I nurturing and strengthening my connections with family, friends, and loved ones?**

The relationships I want to nurture are: _____

The actions I can take to strengthen these connections include: _____

_____

The desired outcomes for these relationships are: _____

_____

❏ **Am I spending quality time with those who matter to me, expressing gratitude, or resolving any lingering issues?**

The specific ways I can spend quality time with loved ones are: _____

_____

The expressions of gratitude I need to make are: _____

_____

The issues I need to resolve are: _____

_____

❏ **Have I worked on healing relationships by seeking or offering forgiveness, making amends, and resolving any conflicts or regrets?**

The relationships I need to heal include: _____

The amends I need to make are: _____

The conflicts or regrets I need to resolve are: _____

3. HEALTH: PRIORITIZING PHYSICAL WELL-BEING

❑ **Am I prioritizing my physical well-being by managing any health conditions, maintaining a healthy lifestyle, and addressing any medical issues?**

The health conditions I need to manage are: _____

_____

The healthy lifestyle habits I want to maintain include: _____

The medical issues I need to address are: _____

_____

❑ **Have I explored alternative therapies or wellness practices that bring comfort and peace?**

The alternative therapies or wellness practices I want to explore include: _____

_____

The comfort or peace I hope to achieve through these practices is: _____

_____

4. SPIRITUALITY: DEEPENING SPIRITUAL PRACTICE

❑ **Am I deepening my spiritual practice, whether through meditation, prayer, reflection, or connecting with a faith community?**

The spiritual practices I want to deepen include: _____

The faith community I want to connect with is: _____

The impact I hope to achieve through these practices is: _____

_____

❑ **If I don't have a faith or belief, how am I connecting to something outside of myself?**

The ways I can connect to something greater than myself include: _____

_____

The feelings or experiences I hope to cultivate are: _____

_____

❑ **Have I explored what brings me peace, comfort, and a sense of purpose or connection to something greater than myself?**

The sources of peace, comfort, and purpose I want to explore are: _____

_____

The sense of connection I hope to achieve is: _____

5. DISCOVERY AND ADVENTURE: EMBRACING LIFE FULLY

❑ **Am I embracing the spirit of adventure by pursuing experiences that bring joy, excitement, or fulfillment?**

The adventures or experiences I want to pursue include: _____

The feelings of joy, excitement, or fulfillment I hope to experience are: _____

_____

❑ **Am I engaging in creative pursuits that allow me to express my thoughts, emotions, and experiences?**

The creative pursuits I want to engage in include: _____

The thoughts, emotions, or experiences I want to express are: _____

_____

❑ **Am I continuing to grow intellectually and emotionally by exploring new ideas, taking up hobbies, or engaging in stimulating activities?**

The new ideas, hobbies, or activities I want to explore include: _____

_____

The intellectual and emotional growth I hope to achieve is: _____

_____

6. TYING UP LOOSE ENDS: ENSURING EVERYTHING IS IN ORDER

Legal Documents:

❏ Have I double-checked that my will, power of attorney, health care directives, and other legal documents are up to date and reflect my current wishes?

The documents I need to review include: _____

_____

The updates or changes I need to make are: _____

_____

The location where these documents are stored is: _____

Financial Accounts:

❏ Have I ensured that my financial accounts, including bank accounts, retirement accounts, insurance policies, and beneficiary designations, are in order and clearly documented?

The accounts I need to review include: _____

The beneficiaries I need to update or confirm are: _____

_____

The location where account details and access information are stored is: _____

_____

End-of-Life Plans:

❏ Have I reviewed and organized all my end-of-life plans, including funeral arrangements, so that my loved ones have clear guidance?

The plans or arrangements I need to confirm include: _____

_____

The specific wishes or instructions I need to document are: _____

_____

The location where these plans are documented is: _____

_____

Document Storage and Access:

❏ Have I communicated where all important documents and information are stored so
my loved ones can easily access them when needed?

The location where documents are stored is: _____

_____

The person(s) who should have access to these documents is/are: _____

_____

The location where access instructions or keys are is: _____

_____

7. LEGACY AND IMPACT: CREATING A LASTING INFLUENCE

❏ **Have I considered the legacy I want to leave behind?**

The legacy I want to create includes: _____

The values or messages I want to pass on are: _____

_____

❏ **Have I been documenting my life stories, writing letters to loved ones, or making
contributions (time or money) to causes I care about?**

The life stories or letters I want to document are: _____

_____

The causes I want to contribute to are: _____

_____

❏ **How do I see myself making my legacy every moment?**

The daily actions or choices that contribute to my legacy are: _____

_____

The impact I hope to have on others is: _____

_____

8. JOY AND PRESENCE: FOCUSING ON THE PRESENT MOMENT

❏ **Am I focusing on being present in the moment and finding joy in simple things?**

The simple things that bring me joy are: _____

_____

The mindfulness practices I want to focus on include: _____

_____

❏ **Am I practicing mindfulness and savoring everyday pleasures to bring a deeper sense of contentment and fulfillment?**

The everyday pleasures I want to savor include: _____

_____

The contentment and fulfillment I hope to achieve are: _____

_____

_____

❏ **Have I experienced greater connection to life by being present to simple and daily joys?**

The simple and daily joys that connect me to life are: _____

_____

The deeper connections I've experienced are: _____

_____

❏ **Have I planned a celebration?**

Here's what I will do: _____

_____

_____

_____

_____

_____

_____

_____

_____

Conclusion

Just as I was finishing up the manuscript for this book, I received an email from a woman who was a coaching client of mine many years ago. The subject line of the email was "Lisa Myers Farewell Tour."

I was puzzled by the subject line, but also quite curious. I'd been lucky enough to coach Lisa previously on a few of her quirky and meaningful creative projects—like the time she wanted to create buttons that said, "Be You" and pass them out to people on the street in order to remind people of the importance of being ourselves in the world. Every interaction I'd ever had with Lisa was touching, heartfelt, and interesting, so I eagerly opened her email.

It turns out that Lisa had been suffering with uterine cancer and had chosen to forgo most treatment in order to preserve her quality of life. She had been scheduled for surgery, but the doctors were unable to proceed due to serious risks of a stroke or fatality. "Thus," Lisa wrote, "I signed up for home hospice, and in true Lisa Myers fashion, decided to embark on the Lisa Myers Farewell Tour."

Lisa explained further: "I decided to contact important people who have been my mentors for writing and for living a good life. I'm reaching out because you've had a great impact on my life, and you were the first person I thought of when I decided to do my farewell tour in the form of live, in-person *Love Lists*. I'm beyond grateful for the chance to share with people what they've meant to me."

Lisa asked if we could schedule a Zoom call. She added, "I've chosen September twenty-seventh as my date for departure. Fortunately New Mexico is a state that has Medical Aid In Dying."

My eyes filled with tears as I read that email from Lisa. I had no idea she was ill, and the last time we'd interacted had been a lively email exchange a couple years earlier following some coaching sessions for Lisa's "Project Gratitude," in which she was writing appreciation letters to musicians and authors who had impacted her life. I simply couldn't imagine a world without this generous, creative, open-hearted person who had brought so much light and love into my life whenever we interacted.

And while I felt so sad about her imminent death, I also felt a swirl of joy. Leave it to Lisa to create a beautiful, loving, meaningful project out of her death! Leave it to Lisa to depart this world in a flurry of live *Love Lists*!

We scheduled a time as soon as we could. Then, Lisa and I spent an amazing two hours together on a Zoom call. We both wore our "Be You" buttons from her loving campaign years previously; she shared some photos of herself and read some of her writing to me. But mostly, we verbalized all the things we loved about each other and talked about what matters most in life.

Lisa revealed, "If I could shout anything from the rooftop right now, it would be that what matters most in life are our connections to the people we love. We have to be more vulnerable and willing to express our love and appreciation. In the end, it is all that counts."

Lisa continued, "Can you imagine how many people have given and received *Love Lists* because of you and your book, *Say It Now*? It doesn't cost anything, and the rewards are immeasurable. It's a simple concept, but it's earth-shattering." She said she'd written a lot of "*Love Lists*," but that now she was getting so much joy out of saying them out loud to people in her life.

Lisa told me during our call that she was feeling strangely blessed to know the day she would die. Knowing the date gave her this opportunity to say goodbye to many people she has loved along the way. In fact, she said she was feeling happier than she had in a long time.

Just a tiny percentage of us know the exact day we will die. However, we all know that we will die.

What if we all took a page from Lisa's book and allowed ourselves to be vulnerable enough and generous enough to write or record or say out loud our *Love Lists* to the people who have impacted us most? What if we chose to make our end of life—from now until our very last moment—truly count?

Brad Wolfe, founder of Reimagine, says, "End of life isn't just logistical or medical. It touches the arts as well as our spirituality, social connections, and community life. No one owns this experience, so we can shape it in ways that truly resonate with us, drawing from all these aspects of our lives."

He continued, "When it comes to planning for the end of life, the sky's the limit. We can get creative and imagine—or reimagine—what this experience can be. What do you want for yourself, your family, and your community? No matter what age you are right now, I invite and encourage you to explore how you want to live fully through the end of your life, until the very last breath."

Lisa is doing exactly what Brad is talking about: She's bringing her creativity and social connections together to imagine a way of dying that is meaningful and that brings her great happiness. She's choosing to *live fully* in the ways that matter most to her, until her last moment on earth.

When I appreciated Lisa for how she has been through all of this, for her creativity, vision and vulnerability, Lisa replied, "Yes, but I figure, what do I have to lose? I'm dying."

When she said that, it made me think, "What do any of us have to lose? We're all dying." But we just don't think of it that way. What if we did? What if we could remember that our time on this planet is limited and that we don't know how many days or months or years we have left? What if we were fully aware that everyone we love will die, and likely sooner than we hope?

How would we choose to live our lives?

You, my friend, my dear reader of this book, have been doing exactly that. Every single action step you have taken through the journey of this workbook is a ripple of love. Every notarized legal paper, every item marked with someone's name, every *Love List* has been an intentional way of shaping a generous life—and of planning a loving death.

I'm so proud of you. What will you do to celebrate yourself, the people you love, and your beautiful life?

Scan Me

Meet Lisa. Watch a video snippet from the special call I got to have with her during the "Lisa Myer Farewell Tour." You can also learn more about her "Be You" project and hopefully be inspired to find new ways to live authentically like *yourself*! Also, listen to an audio from me just for *you*—a celebration of who you are and the way you are choosing to live your life!

Resource Directory

Important Information about this Resource Directory:

We've curated these resources with care, hoping they provide useful guidance and support for you along your journey. The author has used and benefited from many of these resources, however, she can't make any promises about the outcomes you might experience.

Please use your own judgment to ensure books and services are right for you. We aim for accuracy and excellence, and we apologize in advance for any changes that happen between the printing of this book and when it finds its way into your hands. The QR code at the end of this directory will take you to the most updated version!

Your use of this directory is at your own discretion—so, take what works for you, proceed thoughtfully, and remember that there are many other resources out there to support you. New ones are being created every day.

Meet the Experts Quoted in this Book

Alison Luterman
Award winning poet, essayist, and playwright
www.alisonluterman.net

Allen Klein
Author and speaker
https://www.allenklein.com

Babe Hoffarber Garcia
Director of Influencer Marketing at GrowthDay

Brad Wolfe
Founder of Reimagine
www.letsreimagine.org

Brendon Burchard
High Performance Coach, best-selling author, founder of GrowthDay
www.Growthday.com

Carolyn
Community member who is passionate about living life to the fullest and end-of-life planning

Cheri Huber
American teacher of Zen Buddhism, author, founder of Living Compassion
www.LivingCompassion.org

Cheryl Espinosa Jones
Grief counselor, radio host and speaker
www.goodgriefwithcheryl.com

Cynthia Cummins
San Francisco Realtor and Podcast Host
www.kindredsfhomes.com
www.realestatetherapy.org/about

Dianne Myhre
Community member who is passionate about end-of-life planning

Douglas Anderson
Psychologist and community member who is passionate about mindfulness and compassionate living.

Emily Thiroux Threatt
Founder of Grief and Happiness Alliance, author, and podcast host
https://www.griefandhappiness.com/

Flavia Berys
Estate Planning and Real Estate Attorney
www.BerysLaw.com

Gail Trunick
Artist and Founder of Trunick Gallery
www.gailtrunick.com

Greg McKeown
Author of the New York Times bestsellers, "Essentialism" and "Effortless."
www.gregmckeown.com

Jo-Anne Haun
Co-founder of the Death Doula Network of B.C.
www.ddnint.com

Kat Primeau
Artist, educator, and Good Grief Doula
www.goodgriefdoula.com

Kayne Belul
Community member (my son!) who is passionate about decluttering

Lisa Pahl
Hospice Social Worker and co-creator of The Death Deck
www.thedeathdeck.com

Maria Fraietta
Founder and CEO of Nokbox
www.thenokbox.com

Michelle Huljev
MDH Coaching & Consulting
www.mdhcoaching.com

Morgan Oaks
Transformational speaker and Certified High Performance Coach
www.drmorganoaks.com

Paul Wesselmann
Author, speaker, The Ripples Guy
www.theripplesguy.com

Phil Schroeder
Lutheran Pastor and community member who is passionate about end-of-life planning

Rachel Schroeder
Community member who passionate about creativity, relationships, and end-of-life planning

Roy Remer
Executive Director, Zen Caregiving Project
www.zencaregiving.org

Sam Bridgstock
Friend and podcast guest of Greg McKeown
The Greg McKeown Podcast, episode no. 310 + 311, 27 June 2024
www.gregmckeown.com

Sara Zeff Geber
Author of "Solo Aging," professional speaker, and certified retirement coach
https://sarazeffgeber.com

Shawn Buttner
High Performance Coach and Podcaster
www.shawnbuttner.com

Suki Haseman
Community member who is passionate about creativity, relationships, and living life to the fullest

Introduction (General Resources)

AARP (American Association of Retired Persons)
AARP offers guidance on legal, financial, and healthcare considerations, including advance directives and power of attorney.
Visit the website: www.aarp.org/caregiving

The Conversation Project
This initiative is dedicated to helping people talk about their wishes for end-of-life care, encouraging conversations between loved ones and providing resources to ensure that individuals' care preferences are understood and respected when it matters most.
Visit the website: www.theconversationproject.org/

Death Cafe
This global movement brings people together in informal gatherings to discuss death, share stories, and increase awareness of end of life issues, all with the aim of helping people make the most of their lives.
Visit the website: www.deathcafe.com

The Death Deck/Lisa Pahl
The Death Deck is a unique and engaging card game designed to spark meaningful conversations about death and dying. With a mix of humor and thought-provoking questions, this game encourages players to explore their thoughts, fears, and wishes surrounding end-of-life topics in a relaxed, open environment. It's a creative way to break the taboo around death and foster deeper discussions with friends and family. As a Licensed Clinical Social Worker with over seventeen years of experience in hospice and seven years in emergency medicine, Lisa helps people cope with illness, dying, and grief.
Visit the website: www.thedeathdeck.com

Death of the Party

"Death of the Party" is a unique event series and resource platform that aims to spark open, honest conversations about death, dying, and grief in a social setting. Through creative gatherings, workshops, and discussions, the project encourages participants to confront the realities of death in a supportive, communal environment, helping to reduce fear and stigma around the subject.
Visit the website: www.deathofthepartynyc.org

Death Over Dinner

A platform to help people have meaningful conversations about end-of-life wishes in a relaxed setting.
Visit the website: www.deathoverdinner.org

The Elisabeth Kübler-Ross Foundation

This is a non-profit organization focusing on improving end-of-life care and offering grief support. Their work is inspired by the life of psychiatrist, humanitarian, and hospice pioneer Dr. Elisabeth Kübler-Ross.
Visit the website: www.ekrfoundation.org

End of Life Choices California

This non-profit organization provides education, support, and guidance to individuals and families navigating end-of-life decisions, ensuring that Californians have access to information about all legal end-of-life options, including medical aid in dying.
Visit the website: www.endoflifechoicesca.org

End of Life University

End of Life University is an educational platform that offers podcasts, interviews, courses, and resources on end-of-life topics. Hosted by Dr. Karen Wyatt, the platform aims to provide practical advice, spiritual insight, and thoughtful discussions on death, dying, and grief. It serves as a resource for individuals, caregivers, and professionals seeking to better understand and navigate the end-of-life journey.
Visit the website: www.eoluniversity.com

End Well

End Well is a nonprofit organization dedicated to transforming how the world thinks about, plans for, and experiences the end of life. By fostering interdisciplinary collaboration and innovation, End Well aims to create a cultural shift where end-of-life care is viewed as an essential part of life itself, ensuring that everyone has a dignified and meaningful end-of-life experience.
Visit the website: www.endwellproject.org

Essential Retirement Planning for Solo Agers by Sara Zeff Geber
This book offers vital guidance for single and childless adults, focusing on end-of-life and legacy planning, including financial security, healthcare choices, and creating a meaningful legacy, ensuring a well-prepared and fulfilling later life.
Published by TMA Press. For more details, you can find the book on various online platforms.
Visit the website: https://www.amazon.com/Essential-Retirement-Planning-Solo-Agers/dp/1633537684

International Federation on Ageing (IFA)
The IFA is a global organization that advocates for the rights and well-being of older adults, focusing on issues like healthy aging, age-friendly environments, and policies affecting seniors worldwide.
Visit the website: www.ifa-fiv.org

National Institute on Aging (NIA)
Offers guidance on end-of-life care, legal planning, and grief, especially geared toward older adults and caregivers.
Visit the website: www.nia.nih.gov/health/end-life

Nokbox
Nokbox provides a comprehensive kit designed to help organize important documents and end-of-life plans, making it easier for loved ones to manage personal affairs after death. The kit includes templates for financial information, legal documents, and final wishes, all in one place.
Visit the website: www.nokbox.com

Paul Wesselmann
Paul Wesselmann is a writer, speaker & Rippler whose mission is to help people harness the huge potential of even their smallest actions.
Visit the website: www.TheRipplesGuy.com

Reimagine
Reimagine is all about championing new ways to support people at the end of life with a heart-centered approach. It's about creating opportunities for everyone to experience better endings — and better living all the way through.
Visit the website: www.Letsreimagine.org

WeCroak
This app and platform remind users five times daily of life's impermanence, inspired by a Bhutanese tradition, to encourage mindfulness and reflection.
Visit the website: www.wecroak.com

World Health Organization (WHO)
The WHO provides essential information and guidance on palliative care, end-of-life decision-making, and global policies related to death and dying, aiming to improve quality of life for people with serious illnesses.
Visit the website: www.who.int

Section 1: Legacy of Love (Legal Forms)

Aging with Dignity
This organization is committed to ensuring that every person's end-of-life care honors their personal values and dignity, offering resources like the Five Wishes program to help individuals plan for the future.
Visit the website: www.agingwithdignity.org

American Bar Association's Commission on Law and Aging
This commission focuses on addressing legal issues related to aging, providing resources, policy recommendations, and support for older adults, attorneys, and advocates to ensure that the rights and dignity of older adults are protected.
Visit the website: www.americanbar.org/groups/law_aging

Charles Schwab's Financial Independence Guide for Young Adults
This article underscores the importance of parents helping young adults gain financial independence, emphasizing that in case of an emergency, essential forms like powers of attorney and healthcare directives are crucial for protecting both the young adults and their families.
Visit the article: www.schwab.com/learn/story/helping-young-adults-gain-financial-independence

Cheri Huber
Cheri Huber is a Zen teacher and author known for her compassionate and practical teachings on mindfulness and self-compassion. Her bestselling book, *There Is Nothing Wrong with You: Going Beyond Self-Hate*, helps individuals confront self-criticism and embrace self-acceptance. She founded A Center for the Practice of Zen Buddhist Meditation and developed the Recording and Listening practice to support personal growth. Cheri also created Living Compassion, a project that provides essential support for children in Ndola, Zambia.
www.LivingCompassion.org and www.cherihuber.org

Cheryl Espinosa-Jones, Grief Counselor
Cheryl Espinosa-Jones is a grief counselor, coach, and speaker specializing in helping individuals navigate loss and life transitions. With over 30 years of experience, she is known for her compassionate approach and expertise in guiding people through the emotional complexities of grief. Cheryl hosts the podcast *Good Grief*, where she explores

various facets of loss and healing. She is dedicated to supporting others in transforming grief into an opportunity for growth and deeper understanding.
www.goodgriefwithcheryl.com

Cynthia Cummins, Real Estate Therapy
Cynthia Cummins is a real estate agent and founder of Real Estate Therapy, where she combines her real estate expertise with mindfulness to help clients navigate the emotional challenges of buying or selling a home. Her approach focuses on addressing the psychological aspects of real estate transactions, guiding clients toward informed and peaceful decisions. Cynthia offers a holistic perspective, blending practical advice with personal growth.
Visit the website: www.realestatetherapy.org and www.kindredsfhomes.com

The Death Deck/Lisa Pahl
The Death Deck is a unique and engaging card game designed to spark meaningful conversations about death and dying. With a mix of humor and thought-provoking questions, this game encourages players to explore their thoughts, fears, and wishes surrounding end-of-life topics in a relaxed, open environment. It's a creative way to break the taboo around death and foster deeper discussions with friends and family. As a Licensed Clinical Social Worker with over seventeen years of experience in hospice and seven years in emergency medicine, Lisa helps people cope with illness, dying, and grief.
Visit the website: www.thedeathdeck.com

DoYourOwnWill.com
This online platform offers free tools to create customized legal documents, including wills, living wills, and powers of attorney, empowering individuals to take control of their end-of-life planning and ensure their wishes are legally documented.
Visit the website: www.doyourownwill.com

Five Wishes
An easy-to-use advance directive form that addresses medical, emotional, and spiritual wishes.
Visit the website: www.fivewishes.org

Flavia Berys
Flavia Berys is an Estate Planning and Real Estate Attorney licensed in California and Nevada. She also owns a real estate brokerage, offering clients expert legal and real estate services. With her extensive knowledge in estate planning and real estate, Flavia provides comprehensive support for individuals navigating legal and property-related matters.
Visit the website: www.flaviaberys.com

Legal Services Corporation (LSC)
LSC provides access to legal aid services for low-income individuals and families, including assistance with estate planning, advance directives, and end-of-life legal issues.
Visit the website: www.lsc.gov

LegalZoom
LegalZoom offers online legal services, including tools for creating advance healthcare directives, living wills, and other end-of-life planning documents, helping individuals ensure their healthcare and legal wishes are respected during critical moments.
Visit the website: www.legalzoom.com

National Academy of Elder Law Attorneys (NAELA)
This professional association supports attorneys, bar organizations, and others who work with older adults and people with special needs, focusing on elder law and special needs planning to ensure the protection of rights and the promotion of quality of life for these populations.
Visit the website: www.naela.org

Nolo Press
Nolo Press is a leading publisher of self-help legal books and software, offering reliable and easy-to-understand legal information on a wide range of topics, including estate planning, elder law, and end-of-life legal issues.
Visit the website: www.nolo.com

POLST (Physician Orders for Life-Sustaining Treatment) Programs
This resource provides information on state-specific POLST programs, which help ensure that seriously ill patients' treatment preferences are honored across different settings of care, offering a standardized approach to documenting and respecting end-of-life care wishes.
Visit the website: www.polst.org/state-polst-programs

Roy Remer, Executive Director of Zen Caregiving Project
Roy Remer has been an educator and end-of-life caregiver since 1997. As the Executive Director of the Zen Caregiving Project, he integrates mindfulness and compassion into end-of-life care. Roy is also the author of the forthcoming book *Zen Caregiving* (New World Library, Oct. 2025).
Visit the website: www.zencaregiving.org

Section 2: Care and Comforts During Illness (Illness and Hospice)

"Being Mortal: Medicine and What Matters in the End" by Atul Gawande
This bestselling book explores the limitations of modern medicine in addressing the end of life and emphasizes the importance of personal dignity and autonomy in the final stages of life.
Visit the website: www.atulgawande.com/book/being-mortal

Brendon Burchard
Brendon Burchard is a New York Times bestselling author known for his work on personal development and success, world-renowned High Performance Coach, and Founder of GrowthDay. His books, such as *"The Motivation Manifesto"* and *"High Performance Habits,"* focus on helping individuals achieve greater productivity, purpose, and fulfillment in life. Brendon offers practical strategies for mastering motivation, building positive habits, and leading a life of impact and influence.
Visit the website: www.Brendon.com and www.Growthday.com

CaringInfo
A program of the National Hospice and Palliative Care Organization, CaringInfo provides free resources to educate and empower individuals to make informed decisions about serious illness and end-of-life care, ensuring that all people are prepared before a crisis occurs.
Visit the website: www.caringinfo.org

Cheri Huber
Cheri Huber is a Zen teacher and author known for her compassionate and practical teachings on mindfulness and self-compassion. Her bestselling book, *There Is Nothing Wrong with You: Going Beyond Self-Hate*, helps individuals confront self-criticism and embrace self-acceptance. She founded A Center for the Practice of Zen Buddhist Meditation and developed the Recording and Listening practice to support personal growth. Cheri also created Living Compassion, a project that provides essential support for children in Ndola, Zambia.
www.LivingCompassion.org and www.cherihuber.org

Compassion & Choices
This is an organization dedicated to improving care, expanding options, and empowering individuals to make informed decisions about their end-of-life journey.
Visit the website: www.compassionandchoices.org

Cynthia Cummins, Real Estate Therapy

Cynthia Cummins is a real estate agent and founder of Real Estate Therapy, where she combines her real estate expertise with mindfulness to help clients navigate the emotional challenges of buying or selling a home. Her approach focuses on addressing the psychological aspects of real estate transactions, guiding clients toward informed and peaceful decisions. Cynthia offers a holistic perspective, blending practical advice with personal growth.

Visit the website: www.realestatetherapy.org and www.kindredsfhomes.com

Death with Dignity

Death with Dignity promotes the rights of terminally ill individuals to make their own end-of-life decisions, including the option of medical aid in dying.

Visit the website: www.deathwithdignity.org

Eldercare Locator

This public service of the U.S. Administration on Aging connects older adults, caregivers, and families with trustworthy local services and resources, including information on long-term care, support services, and legal aid for aging-related issues.

Visit the website: www.eldercare.acl.gov

"Essentialism: The Disciplined Pursuit of Less" by Greg McKeown

In "Essentialism," Greg McKeown advocates for a focused, disciplined approach to life by identifying and prioritizing what truly matters. The book encourages readers to eliminate non-essential tasks and distractions to achieve greater clarity, productivity, and fulfillment. McKeown offers practical strategies for living with purpose, embracing the power of saying "no," and cultivating a life centered on what is most meaningful.

Visit the website: www.gregmckeown.com/books/essentialism/

Final Exit Network

Final Exit Network provides information and support for individuals seeking to explore their end-of-life options, including medical aid in dying, within legal boundaries.

Visit the website: www.finalexitnetwork.org

Get Palliative Care

Offers resources on palliative care options and ways to manage serious illness for both patients and caregivers.

Visit the website: www.getpalliativecare.org

Hospice Foundation of America

Offers education, resources, and support for those dealing with serious illness and end-of-life care.

Visit the website: www.hospicefoundation.org

International Association for Hospice and Palliative Care (IAHPC)

This global organization is dedicated to advancing hospice and palliative care worldwide, offering resources, education, and advocacy to improve the quality of life for patients with serious illnesses and their families.

Visit the website: www.hospicecare.com/home

Jo-Anne Haun and Karen Hendrickson, Founders of the Death Doula Network International

Jo-Anne and Karen are dying and death Educators, community builders, speakers, and end-of-life doulas. With expertise in coaching, end-of-life care, community death caring, grief, conflict resolution, and communications, they use conversations around dying and death to foster growth and healing for individuals, communities, and the planet.

Visit the website: www.ddnint.com

Michelle Huljev, Life & Executive Coach

Michelle Huljev is a Life and Executive Coach dedicated to helping individuals achieve personal and professional growth. With a focus on mindset, leadership development, and work-life balance, Michelle empowers her clients to overcome obstacles and create meaningful change in their lives and careers. Her coaching approach blends strategic planning with emotional intelligence, guiding clients toward clarity and fulfillment.

Visit the website: www.mdhcoaching.com

National Hospice and Palliative Care Organization (NHPCO)

Provides information on hospice care, advance care planning, and palliative care resources.

Visit the website: www.nhpco.org

Sara Zeff Geber, Ph.D.

Sara Zeff Geber, Ph.D., is the nation's foremost expert on Solo Aging. As an author, professional speaker, and certified retirement coach, she focuses on the unique challenges faced by older adults aging without a partner or children. In 2018, Sara was named an "Influencer in Aging" by PBS' Next Avenue, and she is a regular contributor to Forbes.com on aging and retirement topics.

Visit the website: https://sarazeffgeber.com

Shawn Buttner

Shawn Buttner is a High Performance Coach and the host of the *Meaningful Revolution Podcast*, where he helps creatives and creators sustain their creative impact. Through his coaching, Shawn empowers individuals to achieve peak performance and purpose-driven success in their personal and professional lives.

Visit the website: www.shawnbuttner.com

Tuesdays with Morrie
Written by Mitch Albom, this memoir recounts the life lessons the author learned from his former college professor, Morrie Schwartz, during weekly visits in the final months of Morrie's life. The book explores themes of love, work, community, family, and death, offering profound insights into living a meaningful life.
For more details, you can find the book on various online platforms.

Section 3: When I'm Gone: First Things First (Burial, Cremation, Funerals, etc.)

Allen Klein
Allen Klein is an award-winning speaker, a TEDx presenter, and a best-selling author on the subjects of therapeutic humor. His books include, "Embracing Life After Loss" and "The Healing Power of Humor."
Visit the website: https://www.allenklein.com

Better Place Forests
Better Place Forests offers an alternative to traditional burial by creating memorial forests where individuals can have their ashes spread beneath a dedicated tree, promoting conservation and providing a peaceful, natural setting for end-of-life remembrance.
Visit the website: www.betterplaceforests.com

Coeio (Mushroom Suit)
Coeio offered environmentally-friendly burial solutions, including the Mushroom Suit or Infinity Burial Suit, a biodegradable burial shroud made from mushroom spores. Note: This is the company referred to in Sherry's story, but at the time of publishing, we are not able to confirm that this company is still in business.

Cremation Association of North America (CANA)
CANA provides education and resources on cremation options and trends, helping families make informed decisions about cremation services.
Visit the website: www.cremationassociation.org

Funeral Consumers Alliance (FCA)
The Funeral Consumers Alliance is a non-profit organization dedicated to protecting consumers' rights and promoting transparency in the funeral industry, offering resources and guidance on planning funerals, understanding costs, and making informed end-of-life decisions.
Visit the website: www.funerals.org

The Green Burial Council
The Green Burial Council provides resources and certification for environmentally sustainable burial practices, helping families explore green burial options.
Visit the website: www.greenburialcouncil.org

Legacy.com
Legacy.com provides online obituary and memorial resources, allowing families to create lasting tributes and share memories with loved ones worldwide.
Visit the website: www.legacy.com

The Living Urn
The Living Urn provides biodegradable urns that allow ashes to be planted with a tree, offering an eco-friendly and symbolic option for cremated remains.
Visit the website: www.thelivingurn.com

MyWonderfulLife
MyWonderfulLife helps people create personalized funeral or memorial service plans in advance, ensuring their wishes are honored.
Visit the website: www.mywonderfullife.com

Dr. Morgan Oaks
Dr. Morgan Oaks is a transformational speaker and certified high-performance coach dedicated to helping individuals elevate their greatness. His focus is on empowering people to listen to their intuition and take courageously inspired action to create their best life. Through his coaching and speaking engagements, Dr. Oaks guides individuals toward personal and professional growth by fostering clarity, purpose, and action.
Visit the website: www.drmorganoaks.com

National Funeral Directors Association (NFDA)
NFDA offers comprehensive resources on funeral planning, burial options, and memorial services, as well as guidance on working with funeral directors.
Visit the website: www.nfda.org

The Neptune Society
The Neptune Society specializes in cremation services and offers pre-planning options, including direct cremation and memorial services.
Visit the website: www.neptunesociety.com

Nokbox/Maria Fraietta
Maria Fraietta is the owner and founder of The Nokbox. Nokbox provides a comprehensive kit designed to help organize important documents and end-of-life plans, making it easier for loved ones to manage personal affairs after death. The kit includes templates for financial information, legal documents, and final wishes, all in one place.
Visit the website: www.nokbox.com

Parting
Parting offers a comprehensive directory of funeral homes and cremation providers, allowing families to compare prices and services in their area.
Visit the website: www.parting.com

University of California Body Donation Program
This program allows individuals to donate their bodies to medical education and research, providing essential resources for advancing medical knowledge and training healthcare professionals. Each University of California campus has its own donation program, supporting studies in anatomy, surgery, and disease research.
Visit the website: https://meded.ucsf.edu/willed-body-program
Outside of California: www.anatbd.acb.med.ufl.edu/usprograms

Section 4: Matters of Money, Household, and Your Family's Future (Finances + Household)

1Password
1Password is a password manager that securely stores and manages your passwords, credit card information, and other sensitive data across all your devices. It offers features like encrypted storage, password generation, and secure sharing, making it easier to protect your digital life while keeping everything easily accessible.
Visit the website: www.1password.com

Bitwarden
Bitwarden is an open-source password manager that allows users to store, manage, and share their passwords securely. It offers both free and paid options, with end-to-end encryption.
Visit the website: www.bitwarden.com

Bobby
Bobby is a subscription tracking app that allows users to manually enter and track all their subscriptions in one place, sending reminders when bills are due.
Visit the website: www.bobbyapp.co

Building Your Money Machine by Mel Abraham
This book guides readers through the process of creating a sustainable and scalable business that not only generates ongoing income but also builds a lasting legacy. Mel Abraham emphasizes the importance of developing systems that allow entrepreneurs to achieve financial independence while leaving a positive impact that endures beyond their business, ensuring both personal fulfillment and a meaningful contribution to future generations.
Visit the website: www.melabrahamtraining.com/yourmoneymachinebook

Dashlane

Dashlane provides a secure platform for password storage and management, with features like dark web monitoring, VPN access, and password breach alerts.
Visit the website: www.dashlane.com

LastPass

LastPass offers both free and premium versions for managing passwords, including features like secure password sharing, encrypted storage, and automatic password generation.
Visit the website: www.lastpass.com

Section 5: Clutter Clearing and Memory Keeping (Organizing)

Be More with Less

Be More with Less, created by Courtney Carver, focuses on simplifying life through decluttering, minimalism, and living with intention. It offers resources like blogs and courses for those seeking a clutter-free lifestyle.
Visit the website: www.bemorewithless.com

Everplans

Everplans is a digital platform that helps families plan funerals and memorial services, as well as organize important documents and preferences for end-of-life planning.
Visit the website: www.everplans.com

Forever Photo Organization

Forever offers tools and services for organizing, storing, and preserving your photos and memories. With a focus on permanence, Forever ensures that your photos are safely stored for generations, providing options for organizing, sharing, printing, and converting old media into digital formats. The platform is designed to help you keep your memories secure and easily accessible.
Visit the website: www.forever.com

"The Gentle Art of Swedish Death Cleaning: How to Free Yourself and Your Family from a Lifetime of Clutter" by Margareta Magnusson

In this practical and thoughtful book, Margareta Magnusson introduces the Swedish concept of "döstädning," or death cleaning, which involves decluttering and organizing one's belongings in preparation for the end of life. Magnusson offers gentle advice on how to simplify your living space to reduce the burden on loved ones, while reflecting on the emotional and practical aspects of letting go of possessions.
Visit the website: www.margaretamagnusson.com/books/swedish-death-cleaning

The Gentle Art of Swedish Death Cleaning on Peacock
This show, inspired by Margareta Magnusson's bestselling book, follows individuals who are guided through the process of "Swedish Death Cleaning," which involves decluttering their lives and homes to prioritize what truly matters and strengthen relationships before it's too late.
Visit the website: www.peacocktv.com/stream-tv/the-gentle-art-of-swedish-death-cleaning

Kat Primeau, The "Good Grief Doula"
Kat Primeau, known as the "Good Grief Doula," is an artist and educator who believes in harnessing the transformative power of grief for positive change. Through her work, Kat supports individuals and communities in navigating loss, helping them find growth, healing, and creativity in the grieving process. Her approach blends artistry and education to guide others through the emotional landscape of grief.
Visit the website: www.goodgriefdoula.com

Legacybox
Legacybox is a service that helps you digitize and preserve your old media, such as photos, videos, film reels, and audio recordings. By sending your items to Legacybox, you receive digital copies that are easy to store, share, and enjoy, ensuring that your precious memories are preserved for future generations in a modern format.
Visit the website: www.legacybox.com

Marie Kondo – KonMari Method
Marie Kondo's KonMari Method focuses on decluttering by category, keeping only items that "spark joy." Her books and Netflix series provide guidance for organizing spaces and simplifying life.
Visit the website: www.konmari.com

Nobody Wants Your Parents' Stuff
This article on Next Avenue explores the challenges many people face when dealing with the possessions left behind by their parents. It discusses the emotional and practical difficulties of downsizing and the generational differences in valuing material possessions. The piece provides insights and advice on how to navigate these often difficult conversations and decisions.
For more details, visit the article: www.nextavenue.org/nobody-wants-parents-stuff/

Nokbox/Maria Fraietta
Maria Fraietta is the owner and founder of The Nokbox. Nokbox provides a comprehensive kit designed to help organize important documents and end-of-life plans, making it easier for loved ones to manage personal affairs after death. The kit includes templates for financial information, legal documents, and final wishes, all in one place.
Visit the website: www.nokbox.com/

Shawn Buttner
Shawn Buttner is a High Performance Coach and the host of the *Meaningful Revolution Podcast*, where he helps creatives and creators sustain their creative impact. Through his coaching, Shawn empowers individuals to achieve peak performance and purpose-driven success in their personal and professional lives.
Visit the website: www.shawnbuttner.com

Section 6: Life Lessons and Wisdom I'd Like to Pass On to My Loved Ones (Story Telling)

Allen Klein
Allen Klein is an award-winning speaker, a TEDx presenter, and a best-selling author on the subjects of therapeutic humor. His books include, "Embracing Life After Loss" and "The Healing Power of Humor."
Visit the website: https://www.allenklein.com

Brendon Burchard
Brendon Burchard is a New York Times bestselling author known for his work on personal development and success, world-renowned High Performance Coach, and Founder of GrowthDay. His books, such as *"The Motivation Manifesto"* and *"High Performance Habits,"* focus on helping individuals achieve greater productivity, purpose, and fulfillment in life. Brendon offers practical strategies for mastering motivation, building positive habits, and leading a life of impact and influence.
Visit the website: www.brendon.com and www.growthday.com

Gail Trunick, Founder of Trunick Gallery
Gail Trunick is an artist and the founder of Trunick Gallery, where she showcases her unique, nature-inspired sculptures and artwork. Her creative vision reflects a deep connection to the natural world, with pieces that often incorporate organic materials and themes of transformation. Gail's work is known for its emotional depth and artistic innovation, drawing viewers into a contemplative experience.
Visit the website: www.gailtrunick.com

Legacy Kept
Legacy Kept offers a service that helps you capture and preserve personal stories and family histories. Through guided interviews conducted by professional biographers, they create high-quality audio recordings and beautifully bound books that keep your loved ones' memories alive for future generations.
Visit the website: www.legacykept.com

LifeTime Memoirs

LifeTime Memoirs offers a personalized service to capture and preserve an individual's life story in a professionally written, edited, and beautifully bound autobiography. Through a series of interviews conducted by a skilled writer, they create a lasting legacy in the form of a memoir that can be shared with loved ones and passed down through generations.
Visit the website: www.lifetimememoirs.com

Memories In Writing

Memories In Writing offers professional services to help individuals and families create written memoirs and personal histories. Through personalized interviews and skilled writing, they craft compelling narratives that preserve cherished memories, family traditions, and life experiences in beautifully bound books, ensuring that personal legacies are documented and passed down to future generations.
Visit the website: www.memoriesinwriting.com

Shawn Buttner

Shawn Buttner is a High Performance Coach and the host of the *Meaningful Revolution Podcast*, where he helps creatives and creators sustain their creative impact. Through his coaching, Shawn empowers individuals to achieve peak performance and purpose-driven success in their personal and professional lives.
Visit the website: www.shawnbuttner.com/

StoryCorps

StoryCorps is a nonprofit organization dedicated to recording, preserving, and sharing the stories of people from all walks of life. Through personal interviews, StoryCorps captures meaningful conversations between loved ones, which are then archived at the Library of Congress and can be shared with the public, ensuring that these voices and memories are preserved for future generations.
Visit the website: www.storycorps.org

Storyworth

Storyworth is a service that helps you create a treasured keepsake by prompting your loved ones to share their stories through weekly emailed questions. At the end of the year, their stories are compiled into a beautifully bound book, preserving family memories and personal histories for future generations.
Visit the website: www.storyworth.com

Section 7: True Legacy: Last Love Lists (Love Letters)

The 5 Love Languages: The Secret to Love that Lasts

This book by Dr. Gary Chapman explores the five distinct ways people express and experience love: Words of Affirmation, Acts of Service, Receiving Gifts, Quality Time, and Physical Touch. By understanding people's primary love language and speaking it regularly, you can enhance communication, deepen your connection, and foster more fulfilling relationships.

Published by Northfield Publishing. For more details, you can find the book on various online platforms.

Gratitude Journal by Greater Good Science Center

This online guide from the Greater Good Science Center at UC Berkeley offers practical tips for cultivating gratitude and writing meaningful appreciation letters, with insights from scientific studies on the benefits of gratitude.

Visit the website: www.greatergood.berkeley.edu/article/item/how_to_fully_appreciate_your_loving_relationships

The Love List Toolkit by Sherry Richert Belul

This toolkit is designed to help you create personalized *Love Lists*—collections of affirmations, memories, and appreciations for loved ones. It provides templates, prompts, and inspiration to guide you in crafting meaningful and heartfelt messages that can be shared on special occasions or any day to deepen connections.

Visit the website: https://simplycelebrate.net/love

Paul Wesselmann

Paul Wesselmann is a writer, speaker & Rippler whose mission is to help people harness the huge potential of even their smallest actions.

Visit the website: www.TheRipplesGuy.com

PositivePsychology.com – Gratitude Messages, Letters, and Lists

This resource from PositivePsychology.com offers a comprehensive guide on how to write gratitude messages, letters, and lists. It includes practical tips, examples, and prompts to help you express appreciation and strengthen relationships through written communication. The guide also discusses the psychological benefits of expressing gratitude.

Visit the website: www.positivepsychology.com/gratitude-messages-letters-lists

Say It Now: 33 Creative Ways to Say I Love You to the Most Important People in Your Life

This book by Sherry Richert Belul offers practical and heartfelt ideas for expressing love and appreciation to the people who matter most. Through creative prompts and suggestions, it encourages readers to share their feelings and create meaningful connections, emphasizing the importance of saying what matters while you still have the chance. Published by Books That Save Lives.
Visit the website: https://www.amazon.com/Say-Now-Ways-Important-People/dp/1642500356/

Shawn Buttner

Shawn Buttner is a High Performance Coach and the host of the *Meaningful Revolution Podcast*, where he helps creatives and creators sustain their creative impact. Through his coaching, Shawn empowers individuals to achieve peak performance and purpose-driven success in their personal and professional lives.
Visit the website: www.shawnbuttner.com

Section 8: There's Still Time (Health, Wellness, Spirituality)

Brendon Burchard

Brendon Burchard is a New York Times bestselling author known for his work on personal development and success, world-renowned High Performance Coach, and Founder of GrowthDay. His books, such as *"The Motivation Manifesto"* and *"High Performance Habits,"* focus on helping individuals achieve greater productivity, purpose, and fulfillment in life. Brendon offers practical strategies for mastering motivation, building positive habits, and leading a life of impact and influence.
Visit the website: www.Brendon.com and www.Growthday.com

Emily Thiroux Threatt

Emily Thiroux Threatt is the author of *"Loving and Living Your Way Through Grief,"* *"The Grief and Happiness Handbook,"* and *The Grief and Happiness Cards.* She offers compassionate guidance for navigating grief and finding joy after loss. Emily is also the host of the *Grief and Happiness* podcast, where she explores topics related to healing and living a fulfilling life after loss.
Visit the website: https://lovingandlivingyourwaythroughgrief.com

"Essentialism: The Disciplined Pursuit of Less" by Greg McKeown

In "Essentialism," Greg McKeown advocates for a focused, disciplined approach to life by identifying and prioritizing what truly matters. The book encourages readers to eliminate non-essential tasks and distractions to achieve greater clarity, productivity, and fulfillment. McKeown offers practical strategies for living with purpose, embracing the power of saying "no," and cultivating a life centered on what is most meaningful.
Visit the website: www.gregmckeown.com/books/essentialism

"The Gift of Years: Growing Older Gracefully" by Joan Chittister

In this inspiring book, Joan Chittister offers reflections on the challenges and blessings of aging. With wisdom and grace, she encourages readers to embrace growing older as a time of enrichment, meaning, and spiritual growth. The book is a guide to finding purpose and joy in the later years of life.
Visit the website: www.joanchittister.org

"The Key: And the Name of the Key Is Willingness" by Cheri Huber

This book explores how embracing willingness can unlock personal transformation and mindfulness. Cheri Huber, a Zen teacher, provides simple yet profound insights into how we can overcome resistance, accept our current circumstances, and cultivate a more peaceful life.
Visit the website: www.cherihuber.org

Michelle Huljev, Life & Executive Coach

Michelle Huljev is a Life and Executive Coach dedicated to helping individuals achieve personal and professional growth. With a focus on mindset, leadership development, and work-life balance, Michelle empowers her clients to overcome obstacles and create meaningful change in their lives and careers. Her coaching approach blends strategic planning with emotional intelligence, guiding clients toward clarity and fulfillment.
Visit the website: www.mdhcoaching.com

Dr. Morgan Oaks

Dr. Morgan Oaks is a transformational speaker and certified high-performance coach dedicated to helping individuals elevate their greatness. His focus is on empowering people to listen to their intuition and take courageously inspired action to create their best life. Through his coaching and speaking engagements, Dr. Oaks guides individuals toward personal and professional growth by fostering clarity, purpose, and action.
Visit the website: www.drmorganoaks.com

"Regrets of the Dying" by Bronnie Ware

This book, written by a former palliative care nurse, explores the top regrets people express at the end of their lives. Bronnie Ware shares lessons learned from those she cared for, offering insight into how we can live a more meaningful and fulfilling life by addressing our deepest regrets.
Visit the website: www.bronnieware.com/regrets-of-the-dying

Roy Remer, Executive Director of Zen Caregiving Project

Roy Remer has been an educator and end-of-life caregiver since 1997. As the Executive Director of the Zen Caregiving Project, he integrates mindfulness and compassion into end-of-life care. Roy is also the author of the forthcoming book *Zen Caregiving* (New World Library, Oct. 2025).
Visit the website: www.zencaregiving.org

"A Year to Live: How to Live This Year as If It Were Your Last" by Stephen Levine
In this transformative book, Stephen Levine challenges readers to live each day as if it were their last. Through practical exercises and reflections, Levine encourages a deeper exploration of life, death, and the fear of dying, offering a guide to living more fully and authentically.
Visit the website: www.levinetalks.com

Conclusion

Reimagine
Reimagine is all about championing new ways to support people at the end of life with a heart-centered approach. It's about creating opportunities for everyone to experience better endings — and better living all the way through.
Visit the website: www.Letsreimagine.org

Other Books on Dying and End of Life Planning

"Absolutely Delicious: A Chronicle of Extraordinary Dying" by Alison Jean Lester
In *Absolutely Delicious*, Alison Jean Lester chronicles the extraordinary final months of her mother's life, blending humor, love, and profound reflection on death and dying. Through candid storytelling, Lester captures the challenges and joys of accompanying a loved one through the dying process, offering readers a heartfelt and uplifting perspective on embracing mortality with grace and dignity.
Visit the website: www.alisonjeanlester.com

"Advice for Future Corpses (and Those Who Love Them): A Practical Perspective on Death and Dying" by Sallie Tisdale
In *Advice for Future Corpses*, Sallie Tisdale offers a candid, compassionate, and practical guide to death and dying. Drawing on her experience as a nurse and Buddhist practitioner, Tisdale provides thoughtful insights on how to prepare for death, both for oneself and for loved ones. The book blends humor, wisdom, and realism, addressing the emotional, physical, and spiritual aspects of dying while encouraging readers to confront mortality with openness and grace.
Visit the website: https://www.amazon.com/Advice-Future-Corpses-Those-Love/dp/150118217X

"At Peace: Choosing a Good Death After a Long Life" by Samuel Harrington
In this compassionate guide, Dr. Samuel Harrington addresses the difficult decisions older adults and their families face when considering end-of-life care. He emphasizes the importance of choosing quality of life over aggressive medical interventions, offering advice on how to navigate the healthcare system and make informed choices for a peaceful death.
Visit the website: www.samharrington.com/at-peace

"A Matter of Death and Life" by Irvin D. Yalom and Marilyn Yalom
This moving memoir, co-authored by psychiatrist Irvin Yalom and his wife, Marilyn Yalom, explores their journey through the final months of Marilyn's life following her terminal cancer diagnosis. The book reflects on love, mortality, and the emotional complexities of facing the end of life together.
Visit the website: www.yalom.com/a-matter-of-death-and-life

"Being with Dying: Cultivating Compassion and Fearlessness in the Presence of Death" by Joan Halifax
This book by Zen teacher Joan Halifax provides practical and spiritual guidance for caregivers, patients, and anyone facing the reality of death. Drawing from her decades of work in end-of-life care, Halifax offers practices for cultivating compassion, mindfulness, and fearlessness in the presence of dying, helping readers navigate the emotional and spiritual challenges of mortality.
Visit the website: www.joanhalifax.org

"Die Wise: A Manifesto for Sanity and Soul" by Stephen Jenkinson
In this profound and thought-provoking book, Stephen Jenkinson, a teacher and palliative care worker, explores the concept of dying well in a death-phobic culture. "Die Wise" offers a compassionate and soul-centered approach to facing death with dignity and wisdom. Jenkinson challenges readers to confront their mortality, advocating for a more conscious, meaningful, and community-driven way to approach the end of life.
Visit the website: www.orphanwisdom.com/book/die-wise

"Dying Well: Peace and Possibilities at the End of Life" by Ira Byock
In this compassionate guide, Dr. Ira Byock, a leading palliative care physician, explores how people can approach the end of life with peace and dignity. Byock shares real-life stories of patients and their families, offering insights on how to navigate the emotional and physical challenges of dying while focusing on meaningful connections, comfort, and closure.
Visit the website: www.irabyock.org/books/dying-well

"From Here to Eternity: Traveling the World to Find the Good Death" by Caitlin Doughty
In this fascinating book, Caitlin Doughty embarks on a global journey to explore how different cultures handle death and mourning. Through her travels, Doughty sheds light on unique and meaningful death rituals around the world, challenging the Western approach to death and offering a broader perspective on what it means to die well.
Visit the website: www.caitlindoughty.com/books/from-here-to-eternity

"Goodbye to Clocks Ticking: How We Live While Dying" by Joseph Monninger
In *Goodbye to Clocks Ticking*, author Joseph Monninger offers a deeply personal and poignant memoir about his experience facing a terminal diagnosis. Reflecting on life, love, and mortality, Monninger provides readers with an intimate look at how we can live fully even as we confront the reality of death. This book is both a celebration of life and a meditation on what it means to say goodbye with grace and acceptance.
Visit the website: www.penguinrandomhouse.com/books/718551/goodbye-to-clocks-ticking-by-joseph-monninger

"How We Die: Reflections on Life's Final Chapter" by Sherwin B. Nuland
In this National Book Award-winning work, Dr. Sherwin Nuland offers a frank and compassionate exploration of the physical and emotional processes of dying. Through personal stories and medical insights, Nuland reflects on the realities of death, challenging the notion of a "good death" and emphasizing the importance of understanding and accepting the end of life as part of the human experience.
Visit the website: www.penguinrandomhouse.com/books/122995/how-we-die-by-sherwin-b-nuland

"How We Live is How We Die" by Pema Chödrön
In *How We Live is How We Die*, Pema Chödrön, a renowned Buddhist teacher, offers profound reflections on the natural cycles of life and death, encouraging readers to embrace impermanence with compassion and mindfulness. Through Buddhist teachings, she explores how the way we live shapes our experience of dying and provides guidance on navigating change and uncertainty with grace.
Visit the website: www.pemachodronfoundation.org

"In Love With The World: A Monk's Journey Through the Bardos of Living and Dying" by Yongey Mingyur Rinpoche
In this profound memoir, Tibetan Buddhist master Yongey Mingyur Rinpoche shares his near-death experience and his journey through the bardos—the transitional states between life and death. *In Love With The World* blends spiritual wisdom with a deeply personal narrative, offering readers insights into the nature of existence, the process of dying, and how to live with greater awareness and love. This book serves as both a spiritual guide and a moving reflection on mortality.
Visit the website: https://www.amazon.com/Love-World-Journey-Through-Bardos/dp/0525512543

"It's Always Something" by Gilda Radner
In *It's Always Something*, comedian and original *Saturday Night Live* cast member Gilda Radner shares her deeply personal and humorous account of her battle with ovarian cancer. Through wit, vulnerability, and honesty, Radner reflects on her life, career, and the challenges of facing a serious illness. The memoir captures her unique spirit, offering a message of hope, resilience, and humor even in the face of adversity.

Visit the website: www.simonandschuster.com/books/Its-Always-Something/Gilda-Radner/9781439148860

"I Will Not Die an Unlived Life: Reclaiming Purpose and Passion" by Dawna Markova
In this empowering book, Dawna Markova encourages readers to live with purpose, passion, and authenticity. She reflects on how we can overcome fear, embrace our unique potential, and live fully, regardless of the challenges we face. Markova's inspiring message invites readers to reject the idea of an "unlived life" and to pursue their dreams and passions wholeheartedly.
Visit the website: https://www.dawnamarkova.com

"Man's Search for Meaning" by Viktor E. Frankl
This seminal work by Viktor E. Frankl, a Holocaust survivor and psychiatrist, explores the search for meaning in life, even in the face of suffering and adversity. Drawing from his experiences in Nazi concentration camps, Frankl introduces his philosophy of logotherapy, which emphasizes finding purpose and meaning as a key to survival and personal fulfillment.
Visit the website: www.viktorfrankl.org

"Staring at the Sun: Overcoming the Terror of Death" by Irvin D. Yalom
In this insightful book, renowned existential psychiatrist Irvin D. Yalom delves into the universal fear of death and how it shapes our lives. Drawing from his clinical experience and philosophical insights, Yalom provides guidance on confronting and accepting mortality, offering tools to live a more meaningful life free from the paralyzing fear of death.
Visit the website: www.yalom.com/staring-at-the-sun

"Stiff: The Curious Lives of Human Cadavers" by Mary Roach
In this fascinating and often humorous exploration, Mary Roach delves into the many scientific, medical, and historical roles that human cadavers have played throughout history. From crash test dummies to forensic research, "Stiff" offers a unique and witty look at what happens to our bodies after death, while addressing deeper questions about mortality and the human body.
Visit the website: https://www.amazon.com/Stiff-Curious-Lives-Human-Cadavers-ebook/dp/B00421BN2C

"The Art of Dying Well: A Practical Guide to a Good End of Life" by Katy Butler
This practical guide by Katy Butler offers wisdom on how to live well through the final stages of life. Drawing from personal experience and expert interviews, Butler provides advice on navigating the medical system, making end-of-life decisions, and finding peace as death approaches. The book is a compassionate roadmap for preparing for a graceful and dignified end.
Visit the website: www.katybutler.com/author/the-art-of-dying-well

"The Five Invitations: Discovering What Death Can Teach Us About Living Fully" by Frank Ostaseski

In this profound book, Frank Ostaseski, a renowned Buddhist teacher and hospice co-founder, shares five principles, or "invitations," that death can teach us about living a more meaningful and fulfilled life. Drawing on his extensive experience with the dying, Ostaseski offers wisdom on embracing life's impermanence, fostering compassion, and living with greater awareness and presence.
Visit the website: www.fiveinvitations.com

"The In-Between: Unforgettable Encounters During Life's Final Moments" by Hadley Vlahos

Written by a hospice nurse, this book shares powerful and heartwarming stories of patients during their final days. Hadley Vlahos offers a compassionate and touching look into the profound moments that occur between life and death, revealing the wisdom and peace often found at the end of life.
Visit the website: www.nursehadley.com/book

"The Tibetan Book of Living and Dying" by Sogyal Rinpoche

This spiritual classic blends Tibetan Buddhist wisdom with practical guidance on life and death. Sogyal Rinpoche offers profound insights into the nature of mortality, providing a comprehensive guide to spiritual growth, compassionate living, and preparing for death. The book emphasizes the importance of mindfulness, meditation, and understanding the dying process.
Visit the website: www.rigpa.org/the-tibetan-book-of-living-and-dying

"When Breath Becomes Air" by Paul Kalanithi

This poignant memoir, written by neurosurgeon Paul Kalanithi as he faced terminal lung cancer, explores the meaning of life and death. Kalanithi reflects on his journey from doctor to patient, offering profound insights into mortality, purpose, and what it means to live fully even in the face of death.
Visit the website: https://www.penguinrandomhouse.com

"Who Dies?: An Investigation of Conscious Living and Conscious Dying" by Stephen Levine and Ondrea Levine

This insightful book explores the spiritual and emotional aspects of death and dying, encouraging readers to embrace death as a natural part of life. Stephen and Ondrea Levine offer tools for conscious living and dying, emphasizing the importance of acceptance, compassion, and mindfulness in facing mortality.
Visit the website: https://www.amazon.com/Who-Dies-Investigation-Conscious-Living/dp/0385262213

Books + Resources on Grief for Your Loved Ones

"A Grief Observed" by C.S. Lewis

In this deeply personal work, C.S. Lewis reflects on the grief he experienced following the death of his wife, Joy Davidman. With raw emotion and intellectual depth, Lewis explores the complex feelings of loss, faith, and the challenge of finding meaning in suffering. This book offers a profound and honest portrayal of the grieving process.
Visit the website: www.harpercollins.com/products/a-grief-observed-c-s-lewis

"All the Honey" by Rosemerry Wahtola Trommer

In this beautiful collection of poetry, Rosemerry Wahtola Trommer explores themes of love, loss, joy, and the sweetness of life. Her poems offer a meditative and heartfelt reflection on the everyday moments that make life meaningful, with a focus on finding grace and gratitude even in difficult times.
Visit the website: www.wordwoman.com

"Bittersweet: How Sorrow and Longing Make Us Whole" by Susan Cain

In this insightful book, Susan Cain explores the concept of bittersweetness—the recognition that life is a blend of joy and sorrow. Drawing on research, philosophy, and personal stories, Cain delves into how embracing both the beauty and pain of life can lead to personal growth, creativity, and a deeper sense of connection to the world.
Visit the website: www.susancain.net/book/bittersweet

"Broken Open: How Difficult Times Can Help Us Grow" by Elizabeth Lesser

In this inspiring book, Elizabeth Lesser explores how life's challenges, including loss and grief, can lead to personal transformation and growth. Drawing from her own experiences and the stories of others, Lesser offers wisdom on how to navigate painful times with grace, resilience, and the opportunity to open up to deeper truths about ourselves.
Visit the website: www.elizabethlesser.org/broken-open

Compassionate Friends

Compassionate Friends provides support for families who have lost a child. They offer a nationwide network of support groups, online resources, and bereavement services.
Visit the website: www.compassionatefriends.org

"Embracing Life After Loss" by Allen Klein

In this uplifting book, Allen Klein offers guidance on how to find joy and meaning after experiencing loss. Through personal stories, humor, and wisdom, Klein provides readers with tools to embrace life again, even in the midst of grief. The book encourages healing through acceptance, laughter, and a renewed sense of purpose.
Visit the website: https://www.amazon.com/Embracing-Life-After-Loss-Growing/dp/1642500062

End of Life University

End of Life University is an educational platform that offers podcasts, interviews, courses, and resources on end-of-life topics. Hosted by Dr. Karen Wyatt, the platform aims to provide practical advice, spiritual insight, and thoughtful discussions on death, dying, and grief. It serves as a resource for individuals, caregivers, and professionals seeking to better understand and navigate the end-of-life journey.
Visit the website: www.eoluniversity.com

"Giving Grief Meaning" by Lily Dulan

Lily Dulan's book offers a compassionate approach to transforming grief into healing. After the devastating loss of her daughter, Lily created the "Love and Light" method, which provides practical tools for finding meaning and connection in the aftermath of loss. The book encourages readers to work through their grief with love, mindfulness, and intentional practices.
Visit the website: https://www.amazon.com/Giving-Grief-Meaning-Transforming-Suffering/dp/1642503134

"Grief Recovery Handbook: The Action Program for Moving Beyond Death, Divorce, and Other Losses" by John W. James and Russell Friedman

This practical guide offers a structured approach to dealing with various forms of grief. Through actionable steps, the authors provide a framework to help individuals work through their loss and begin healing.
Visit the website: www.griefrecoverymethod.com

GriefShare

GriefShare is a network of support groups for people grieving the death of a loved one. They offer in-person and online support groups that meet regularly, providing a supportive community to help individuals navigate the grief process.
Visit the website: www.griefshare.org

"It's OK That You're Not OK: Meeting Grief and Loss in a Culture That Doesn't Understand" by Megan Devine

Megan Devine challenges conventional wisdom about grief in this thoughtful book, offering validation and support for those grieving in a world that often misunderstands the process. She advocates for a more compassionate approach to mourning.
Visit the website: www.refugeingrief.com/books/its-ok-that-youre-not-ok

"Loving and Living Your Way Through Grief: A Comprehensive Guide to Healing from Loss" by Emily Thiroux Threatt
In this heartfelt guide, Emily Thiroux Threatt shares her personal journey of loss and offers practical advice on how to navigate the grieving process. The book encourages readers to embrace love and self-compassion while working through grief, offering tools for healing and finding a path forward after loss.
Visit the website: https://www.amazon.com/Loving-Living-Your-Though-Grief/dp/1642504823

"Modern Loss: Candid Conversation About Grief. Beginners Welcome." by Rebecca Soffer and Gabrielle Birkner
This insightful and often humorous book offers a modern take on grief, featuring personal stories, practical advice, and candid discussions about the experience of loss. Rebecca Soffer and Gabrielle Birkner provide a relatable and compassionate guide for navigating grief in today's world, making it accessible and less isolating.
Visit the website: www.modernloss.com

National Alliance for Grieving Children (NAGC)
The NAGC connects children and families with grief support programs across the country. They offer a directory of local bereavement programs and resources for those grieving the loss of a loved one.
Visit the website: www.childrengrieve.org

"No Time to Say Goodbye: Surviving the Suicide of a Loved One" by Carla Fine
This deeply compassionate book offers support for those grieving the loss of a loved one to suicide. Carla Fine shares her own experiences as well as the stories of others, providing guidance for coping with the unique pain and emotions that follow such a tragic loss.
Visit the website: www.carlafine.com/no_time_to_say_goodbye__surviving_the_suicide_of_a_loved_one_15329.htm

Open to Hope
Open to Hope offers an extensive directory of bereavement groups and grief resources. They provide information on finding support groups, counselors, and other grief-related services.
Visit the website: www.opentohope.com

"Option B: Facing Adversity, Building Resilience, and Finding Joy" by Sheryl Sandberg and Adam Grant

In this powerful book, Sheryl Sandberg, COO of Facebook, and psychologist Adam Grant provide insights on how to build resilience in the face of adversity. Drawing from Sandberg's personal experience with loss and Grant's expertise in psychology, they offer practical advice and stories of people who have overcome life's toughest challenges, emphasizing the importance of resilience and finding joy after tragedy.
Visit the website: www.optionb.org

"Postal Service for the Dead" by Sleepy Sue Studio

"Postal Service for the Dead" is a unique project that allows people to send letters to their deceased loved ones. The service provides a space for those grieving to express their feelings, process loss, and maintain a connection through the act of writing. Each letter is treated with care and confidentiality, offering a therapeutic way to communicate with the departed.
Visit the website: www.sleepysue.studio/postal-service-for-the-dead

"Rebellious Mourning: The Collective Work of Grief" edited by Cindy Milstein

This powerful anthology explores the intersection of grief and social justice, highlighting how collective mourning can be a catalyst for resistance and social change. Through essays, stories, and reflections, contributors reveal how grief can be harnessed to challenge injustice and build community. "Rebellious Mourning" calls for a rebellion against societal norms that suppress grief, urging readers to embrace mourning as a transformative force.
Visit the website: www.akpress.org/rebellious-mourning.html

"Tear Soup: A Recipe for Healing After Loss" by Pat Schwiebert and Chuck DeKlyen

This beautifully illustrated book uses the metaphor of making soup to explore the process of grieving. It's an excellent resource for both adults and children, offering comfort and understanding for those going through loss.
Visit the website: www.griefwatch.com/collections/tear-soup-home

Telephone of the Wind

The Telephone of the Wind is a symbolic and therapeutic project offering a unique way for people to communicate with loved ones who have passed away. Inspired by the original Japanese wind telephone, this project provides a space for visitors to express their grief, share memories, and find solace by "speaking" to the deceased through an unconnected rotary phone. The experience allows for a meaningful, reflective connection in a peaceful environment.
Visit the website: www.thetelephoneofthewind.com

The Dougy Center
The Dougy Center offers grief support resources for children, teens, and families. They provide directories and tools to find local bereavement support groups as well as resources for supporting individuals through grief.
Visit the website: www.dougy.org

"The Grieving Brain: The Surprising Science of How We Learn from Love and Loss" by Mary-Frances O'Connor
In this fascinating book, neuroscientist Mary-Frances O'Connor explores the science of grief, explaining how the brain processes loss and why grieving is a natural part of life. The book provides a deeper understanding of the biological and emotional aspects of grief.
Visit the website: www.maryfrancesoconnor.org/books/the-grieving-brain

"The Orphaned Adult: Understanding and Coping with Grief and Change After the Death of Our Parents" by Alexander Levy
This book explores the unique grief experienced by adults after the loss of their parents. It provides insights into the emotional and psychological impact of becoming an orphaned adult, with practical advice on coping and healing.
Visit the website: www.goodreads.com/book/show/282967.The_Orphaned_Adult

"The Sudden Loss Survival Guide: Seven Essential Practices for Healing Grief" by Chelsea Hanson
This compassionate guide offers practical advice for coping with the shock and grief of sudden loss. Chelsea Hanson provides readers with seven essential practices to help navigate the overwhelming emotions that come with unexpected loss, offering tools for healing, self-care, and finding peace.
Visit the website: https://www.amazon.com/Sudden-Loss-Survival-Guide-Essential/dp/1642502286

"The Year of Magical Thinking" by Joan Didion
This powerful memoir chronicles Joan Didion's experience of grief following the sudden death of her husband, John Gregory Dunne. With raw honesty and emotional depth, Didion explores the impact of loss, the fragility of life, and the process of mourning in the face of unimaginable tragedy.
Visit the website: www.joandidion.org/joan-didion-books/the-year-of-magical-thinking

"The Wild Edge of Sorrow: Rituals of Renewal and the Sacred Work of Grief" by Francis Weller

In this profound book, Francis Weller explores the transformative power of grief and its importance in healing and personal growth. Blending psychology, anthropology, and spiritual wisdom, Weller offers rituals and practices to help individuals embrace sorrow, navigate loss, and reconnect with the sacred work of grieving.

Visit the website: www.francisweller.net/the-wild-edge-of-sorrow-the-sacred-work-of-grief.html

"When Things Fall Apart: Heart Advice for Difficult Times" by Pema Chödrön

In this beloved book, Buddhist nun Pema Chödrön offers timeless wisdom for navigating life's challenges. With profound insights drawn from Buddhist teachings, she encourages readers to embrace uncertainty and difficult emotions, finding peace and resilience in the midst of pain and chaos. This book provides practical guidance on how to stay open and compassionate during tough times.

Visit the website: https://pemachodronfoundation.org

QR Code: Here is a link to the most updated version of this directory, which includes additional resources for you as they become available.

Scan Me

Here is a link to the most updated version of this directory, which includes additional resources for you as they become available.

Connect with Me!

We've been on a huge and important journey together. I would love to stay in touch with you and would be grateful to hear your stories about this process.

I welcome all reader feedback—what was helpful, what was hard, what impacted you the most, and ways you celebrated yourself along the journey!

You matter to me! Please connect.

Here are some ways to connect and to continue our journey:

- Please post a review on Amazon. Every reader review goes a long way to helping make books like this more accessible to others.

- If you would be willing to post that same review to Goodreads, that would be icing on the cake! I will be active on Goodreads after the book is published so we can continue to support one another to live our best, most loving lives until our very last breath.

- Download the *Love List* Tool Kit and subscribe to my weekly emails and LoveGrams here: simplycelebrate.net/love

- Post your stories, questions, and thoughts on my Simply Celebrate Facebook Page and in my Say it Now Group: www.facebook.com/simplycelebrate www.facebook.com/groups/presentperfectgifts

- Email me: connect@simplycelebrate.net

- Join me on other social media channels, wherever you are: www.instagram.com/simplycelebrate www.youtube.com/sherrybelul www.linkedin.com/in/sherryrichertbelul www.tiktok.com/@simply_celebrate simplycelebrate.bsky.social

Acknowledgments

Writing this book has been a journey I could never have done on my own. Along the way, I've been supported, guided, and inspired by so many amazing people and communities. I'm especially grateful to those who aren't afraid to talk about death and dying, knowing how positive and healing those conversations can be. Thank you for your encouragement and influence—it meant the world to me in bringing this project to life.

Thank you to everyone at Books That Save Lives who contributed to this book. I am deeply grateful for your hard work and dedication.

An extra special thank you to cofounder and publisher of BTSL, Brenda Knight for your countless hours of guidance and consultation. Brenda, you are not only a whip-smart businesswoman but also someone with a heart of gold and electric intuition. Your commitment to your authors is unmatched. You are definitely the book fairy godmother!

Thank you to Joanna Price and to Carmen Fortunato for the care, talent, and joy you put into the book cover and interior design. You brought my words to life!

Thank you to every person I interviewed or quoted in this book. Each of you contributed so much wisdom, heart, and insight. I am deeply appreciative for the ways you are each making the world a better and gentler place: Alison Luterman, Allen Klein, Babe Hoffarber Garcia, Brad Wolfe, Brendon Burchard, Bronnie Ware, Carolyn from Zumba class, Cheri Huber, Cheryl Espinosa Jones, Cynthia Cummins, Dianne Myhre, Douglas Anderson, Emily Thiroux Threatt, Flavia Berys, Gail Trunick, Greg McKeown/Sam Bridgstock, Jo-Anne Haun, Kat Primeau, Kayne Belul, Lisa Nan Myers, Lisa Pahl, Michelle Huljev, Mitch Albom, Morgan Oaks, Nokbox/Maria, Paul Wesselmann, Phil and Sharon Schroeder, Rachel Schroeder, Roy Remer, Sara Zeff Geber, Shawn Buttner, StoryCorps, StoryWorth, and Suki Haseman.

Thank you to Brad Wolfe and the team at Reimagine. Your mission and widespread work are bringing so much compassion and awareness to the world. You inspired me to write this book before I even knew I was writing it.

Thank you to my writer family—Alison Luterman, Kirsten Soares, Laurie Wagner, Maya Stein, and Rosemerry Wahtola Trommer. Your work and hearts inspire me every day.

Thank you to the most amazing and supportive book encourager ever, Tamara Monosoff. Your love, excitement, practical tips, and cheering on have been the biggest boost!

Thank you to Brendon Burchard for teaching me the concept of mortality motivation as a way to make each day truly count.

Thank you to my spiritual guide Cheri Huber—and also to Ashwini and Living Compassion. You have helped me practice letting go in countless ways. You've been my teachers in death and dying—and living fully—for more than thirty years.

Thank you to my closest clan, Bob, Kayne, Ian, Tricia, and Rachel. You never complained about hearing about death and dying at every meal or on every phone call for months on end.

Thank you to my own family's next generation, Tara, Nikki, Kayne, Kinsley, Luka, and LouLou, whom I hope will benefit greatly by the plans your elders make.

Thank you to my mom for being my biggest cheerleader and for your kind and consistent support. You taught me the power of books and you remind me to find simple joys every day by focusing on the people we love.

I also want to acknowledge everyone who has created an end-of-life plan or who will use this book to do so. I deeply respect and admire the courage it takes to face this process head-on. Taking the time to make these plans is an incredibly generous and loving act, one that eases the burden on loved ones and reflects a profound sense of care.

About the Author

Sherry Richert Belul, founder of Simply Celebrate, helps people find creative, intentional, and impactful ways to celebrate life and to express love for family and friends. As a certified life coach, Sherry supports people in living their best lives—lives full of joy, success, engagement, and meaningful relationships. She is the author of *Say It Now: 33 Creative Ways to Say I LOVE YOU to the Most Important People in Your Life*, cohost of the *Heart Wisdom Panel* with Books That Save Lives, and co-founder of *The Secret Agents of Change* kindness project. Her work has been featured in the *New York Times*, *Town & Country*, and the *Wall Street Journal*. Sherry has been interviewed on countless podcasts and has led a variety of workshops in an array of venues ranging from bookstores to large companies.

Sherry teaches that celebration and grief are two sides of the same coin. She helps people navigate loss, illness, and death by fostering meaningful connections and celebrating life's depthful moments. In collaboration with Reimagine, Sherry leads workshops guiding participants in creating *Love Lists* for those who are dying or who have passed away, transforming grief into a celebration of love. She also facilitates Grief + Growth groups through the personal development platform GrowthDay. Her work advocates honest and open conversations about death and dying as a way to live more intentionally. Sherry lives in San Francisco.

Books That Save Lives came into being in 2024 when the editor and publisher, Brenda Knight, heard directly from readers and authors that certain self-help, grief, psychology books, and journals were providing a lifeline for folks. We live in a stressful world where it is increasingly difficult not to feel overwhelmed, worried, depressed, and downright scared. We intend to offer support for the vulnerable, including people struggling with mental wellness and physical illness as well as people of color, queer and trans adults and teens, immigrants and anyone who needs encouragement and inspiration.

From first responders, military veterans, and retirees to LGBTQ+ teens and to those experiencing the shock of bereavement and loss, our books have saved lives. To us, there is no higher calling.

We would love to hear from you! Our readers are our most important resource; we value your input, suggestions, and ideas.

Please stay in touch with us and follow us at:
https://www.booksthatsavelives.net
https://www.instagram.com/booksthatsavelives/
https://www.facebook.com/people/Books-That-Save-Lives/
https://www.youtube.com/@BooksThatSaveLives

www.ingramcontent.com/pod-product-compliance
Lightning Source LLC
Jackson TN
JSHW061759051025
91506JS00001B/1